"*Songs in Sepia and Black and White* is about the influences that make us; in these 101 poems Norbert Krapf explores the richness of his ancestry, from the memory of his parents to his abiding, formative love for Walt Whitman, Emily Dickinson, Bob Dylan, and other figures. A book to treasure–and a book that confirms Krapf's status as one of America's finest living poets."

Benjamin Hedin,
editor of *Studio A: The Bob Dylan Reader*

"*Songs in Sepia and Black and White* is a collection that you will want to take with you wherever you travel, even if only to the next room. Norbert Krapf's poetry makes you want to celebrate your own family history, your own roots, and the beauty that surrounds us all."

David Amram,
composer, multi-instrumentalist, author

“The book title for the entire collection very appropriately reflects all three artistic genres of this volume: music, pictorial art (photography), and language as the medium of poetry.”

Gert Niers,
poet and critic, *German Life*

“Krapf is a mature poet at the height of his power.”

Joe Bruchac,
author of multiple poetry books

Songs in Sepia and Black & White

Songs in Sepia and Black & White

Norbert Krapf

Photographs by *Richard Fields*

QUARRY BOOKS
an imprint of
INDIANA UNIVERSITY PRESS
Bloomington & Indianapolis

This book is a publication of

QUARRY BOOKS

an imprint of

INDIANA UNIVERSITY PRESS
601 North Morton Street
Bloomington, Indiana 47404-3797 USA

iupress.indiana.edu

Telephone orders 800-842-6796
Fax orders 812-855-7931

∞ The paper used in this publication meets the minimum requirements of the American National Standard for Information Sciences – Permanence of Paper for Printed Library Materials, ANSI Z39.48-1992.

Manufactured in the United States of America

Library of Congress Cataloging-in-Publication Data

Krapf, Norbert [date]
Songs in sepia and black and white / Norbert Krapf ; photographs by Richard Fields.
p. cm.
ISBN 978-0-253-00632-5 (pb : alk. paper) – ISBN 978-0-253-00636-3 (ebook)
I. Fields, Richard. II. Title.
PS3561.R27S66 2012
811'.54 – dc23
2011053370

1 2 3 4 5 17 16 15 14 13 12

for Annie and Vince Clemente
and Han and Bill Heyen
in memory of
the waters and light
of Walt's Island home

NORBERT KRAPF

for my granddaughters
Clara and Jillian

RICHARD FIELDS

It is the privilege and the labor of the apprentice of creation to come with his imagination into the unimaginable, and with his speech into the unspeakable.

Wendell Berry, "A Native Hill"

All things are inventions of holiness.
Some more rascally than others.

Mary Oliver, "The Wren from Carolina"

Logic and sermons never convince,
The damp of the night drives deeper into my soul.

Walt Whitman, "Song of Myself"

KEUSCH
KUEBLER

Contents

Acknowledgments

Some of the poems in this volume originally appeared, sometimes in different form or with different titles, in the following publications: *A Prairie Journal:* "Orchards"; *Branches:* "Beneath the Stones," "What Remains"; *Flying Island:* "Caveat Emptor"; *From the Edge of the Prairie:* "Bavarian Blue," "Come with Me," "Dogwoods and Rosebuds for Rita," "Downtown Indy Freight Trains," "End of the Path," "Basho's Journey," "Maybe I Knew Him," "Missing the Turn," "Monon Memories," "Mulberry Blues," "Schramm Woods," "The Boy and the Flying Squirrel," "The Family Farm" (section 6 of "The Family Farm: For Wendell Berry"), "Walking to School," "White Knuckles," "Woods Time"; *Indiana German Heritage Society Newsletter:* "Eberhard Reichmann at Peter's Gate"; *Indiana Humanities Council Blog National Poetry Month 2010 Special:* "Rumi for Breakfast"; *The Long Islander:* "Young Hunter's Prayer"; *Oklahoma Today:* "Woody Guthrie's Guitar Machine"; *Sea Stories:* "Basho's Waters," "Moon of Falling Leaves," "Saying Patoka," "The Come Home from the Flood Telegram," "The Float Forever Held," "Walt Whitman on the South Shore"; *The Awakenings Review:* "Dream While My Son Is in the Hospital"; *Tipton Poetry Journal:* "Leaves United for Etheridge Knight at Crown Hill Cemetery," "Patoka Visions," "The Mayberry Café"; *Valparaiso Poetry Review:* "Goodnight, Irene."

"Back in Indiana," "Drifting," "Virgil in Hill Country," and "Wild Onions" first appeared in the anthology *Rivers, Rails, and Runways* (San Francisco Bay Press, 2008) by the Airpoets, Joyce Brinkman, Ruthelen Burns, Joseph Heithaus, Norbert Krapf, and Jeannie Deeter Smith; "Saying Patoka" was reprinted in the anthology *Airmail by the Airpoets* (San Francisco Bay Press, 2011). "A Blank Piece of Paper" first appeared in *An Endless Skyway: Poetry from the State Poets Laureate* (Ice Cube Books, 2011), edited by Caryn Mirriam-Goldberg, Marilyn L. Taylor, Denise Low, and Walter Bargen. "Someone Who Misses New Orleans" originally appeared on the CD with Monika Herzig, *Imagine – Indiana in Music and Words* (Acme Records, 2007); "Looking for Walt Whitman on Campus" and "Mockingbird Memory" were part of the online collection *Campus Meditations* written by the author, in his capacity as Long Island University Poet Laureate, to celebrate the fiftieth anniversary of the founding of the C.W. Post Campus of LIU; "Prayer to Walt Whitman at Ground Zero" first appeared in William Heyen's anthology *September 11, 2001: American Writers Respond* (Etruscan Press, 2002) and was reprinted in English and German in Helmbrecht Breinig's *Poetischer New York–Führer* (Wissenschaftliche Buchgesellschaft, 2005) and in *Elements of Literature* (Holt, Rinehart and Winston, 2009/2011), a textbook for Grade 11; "Arlo and Bob Go Fishing" was included in Dorothy Alexander's *Travelin' Music: A Poetic Tribute to Woody Guthrie* (Village Books Press, 2010).

"Girl of the Hill Country" appeared in *Sweet Sister Moon* (WordTech Editions, 2009) and is reprinted by permission; "I'm Practically with the Band" and "The Fiddler" appeared in *Bloodroot: Indiana Poems* (Indiana University Press, 2008). The author thanks the Airpoets, named above, for their suggestions on some of these poems. The author and photographer thank editor Linda Oblack for supporting this book, and two others, above and beyond the call of duty, and wish her a lively retirement in which she keeps busy being born. They also thank Riley Fields for his photographs of Norbert's poem in the Martin Donlin stained-glass panel at the new Indianapolis International Airport, the Walt Whitman Birthplace in Huntington Station (West Hills), Long Island, and the surf and sand at Jones Beach. Thanks to Janet Werne and Mike Schmitt for opening gates in St. Henry and Ireland, Indiana, Tim Grimm for including the author in the Hoosier Dylan show, and Gordon Bonham, Jennie DeVoe, Jason Wilber, Bobbie Joe Lancaster, and the other fine Indiana musicians who provided musical backing onstage and camaraderie backstage. Thanks also to Monika Herzig, girl of the Swabian hill country, for thinking of combining poetry and jazz, and to her husband Peter Kienle for breaking loose one winter night on the guitar in southern Indiana. Finally, special thanks to Anne Valentine, Shannon Linker, and Dave Lawrence, Arts Council of Indianapolis, for the Creative Renewal Fellowship to combine poetry and music, with an emphasis on the blues.

Songs in Sepia and Black & White

1 *Songs in Sepia and Black & White*

Songs in Sepia and Black and White

There was a handsome man who
parted his hair down the middle,
a man who left way too young.

Died at thirty-three, father
of six, the eldest only twelve.
This man played the mandolin,

sang German songs as a tenor.
I sometimes see him in sepia,
sometimes in black and white.

I sing fire sage for Dorothy,
miniature irises and roses
climbing a white trellis.

Shallots growing in her garden
and rhubarb stalks at the edge.
Lettuces in her cold frame.

Memories of a father who died
when she was six, memories
of a mandolin and tenor voice.

Stories and irises for me, the grandson,
from Frank's late daughter, Dorothy.
Songs in sepia and black and white.

The Kaiser and the Little Girl's Tongue

When she was a little girl during
WW I and wanted to speak German
like the elders she loved,

they would say, "You better not
speak German or the Kaiser
will get your tongue!"

So what happened when
my mother could not stop
herself from singing

Stille Nacht, heilige Nacht,
Silent night, holy night?
Did the Kaiser jump out

from behind the couch
and tie her tongue
in a nasty knot?

Did a tiny red devil
dart a sharp pitchfork
into her tender tongue?

The Come Home from the Flood Telegram

"Are you OK come home,"
wrote the brother to his third
sister in the great Louisville flood
of January 1937 and she came.

Came back across the Ohio River
to the hill country and worked
as a secretary in a lumber company.
A few years later met the man

who became my father. They stayed
home until called into another world.
More than seventy years after the flood
waters receded, the yellow telegram

floats in a drawer of my desk.
After thirty-four years I came
home from New York. Nobody
sent me a telegram. Home called

in other ways. What if? What if
she had not come back? Had not
listened to the command that must
have come from her mother?

Is there not always a *What if*
whenever there is a flood?
Some heed the call and some
do not. Some know home

as where you must go when they
call you back after your time
in the city. Others know home
as the place you must get beyond,

where you shrivel and die if
you go back. Some ride the waters
and settle wherever they recede
and say they never look back.

Some cut off all ties and face away.
Some go back and look within.
Some close off, some stay open
and ponder *What if* telegrams.

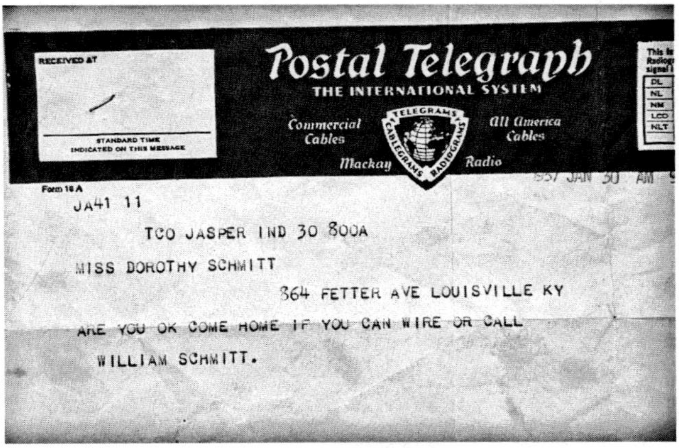

RECEIVED AT

STANDARD TIME INDICATED ON THIS MESSAGE

Postal Telegraph

THE INTERNATIONAL SYSTEM

Commercial Cables — TELEGRAMS CABLEGRAMS RADIOGRAMS — All America Cables

Mackay Radio

DL
NL
NM
LCO
NLT

Form 16 A

937 JAN 30 AM

JA41 11

TCO JASPER IND 30 800A

MISS DOROTHY SCHMITT

364 FETTER AVE LOUISVILLE KY

ARE YOU OK COME HOME IF YOU CAN WIRE OR CALL

WILLIAM SCHMITT.

The Boy in the Saloon

The boy watches the men
who come into the saloon
for a mug of beer and a plate
of sausage, sauerkraut
and mashed potatoes.

He listens for what they
say, watches how when
their mouths open their
faces make changing lines.

Beer foam blesses his lips
when the men offer him sips.
The words that come toward him
hang in the air as if floating
from another world beyond
the one in which they live:
Kartoffel, Schnapps, Deine Mutter,
Dein Vater, Deine Schwester.

Shadows glide from the bar
as beer drips from the tap.
The boy finds himself in laps
that spill into one another
and connect to the stairs
up which he toddles
as an elderly hand leads
him toward a bed onto which
he falls and drifts away above
the bubbles of male laughter
and the singing of songs
that say food and beer are
the *Mutter und Vater* of life.

Be glad you have a family.
Enjoy this life we have
in this new country where
anybody can own a saloon
and doors open into sunlight.

Boy, you have a future.
Alles geht uns hier sehr gut!
Be glad we came here. This
land is our land, *Jawohl.*

The Boy and the Flying Squirrels

Across the road from where he was born,
in a room above a saloon, stood the first

church, built by the German pioneers
who founded the village and parish

during the Civil War. They planted
a row of cedars to grow along both sides

of their new brick church, already too
small by the time he was born, shortly after

the turn of a new century. As a boy, he watched
his relatives take down the bricks of the small

church and make them part of a larger one.
His father, who operated a steam-engine sawmill,

cut the timber for the beams of the new St. Henry
Church, which rose at an angle from the old cedars

they left standing so all could still see the outline
of the old that became part of the fabric of the new.

Today, early in another new century,
those ancient cedars still stand,

but the first church is a phantom
we carry beneath our eyelids.

The boy, whose spirit soared to another world,
watched flying squirrels leap from one cedar

to another across the space where the first
church once stood. That boy was my father,

who told me the story of the flying squirrels.
Over a hundred years later I see the cedars

still standing beside the phantom church,
in the village now grown smaller and quieter.

Invisible squirrels with tails working like angel
wings fly from one cedar bough to another.

Walking to School

This time you are doing it on foot.
You are not going to listen, even
though your father says it's too far
to walk and he can't afford to buy
a horse because there are ten children.

No, no, you are not going to stop
after eighth grade, you are too smart
for that, you can multiply three-figure
numbers in your mind by imagining
them on the blackboard, as the nun
taught you to do in the small
schoolhouse at the edge of the cemetery.
You can speak and read both English
and German because half of each school
day the past eight years was taught
in English, half in German. Not even
a war against the Germans is going
to stop you from going to where
you deserve to go. You can do it.
Don't worry that the language
spoken at home is now *verboten.*

Let the brothers and sisters who don't
want to learn any more stay home.
You burn to learn, you are not going
to stay home, you are not going to listen
to a decision that will stop you.
You are going to get there by foot,
no matter how long it takes, no matter
how early you must leave, how late
you will get back home in winter.
You can do it, you shall do it.

You do not know that your four
children will all graduate from college,
that one will get a Masters, another the Ph.D.

You are doing this for yourself, you deserve
four more years, you have earned it, why
should mere distance hold you back?
Who are you to acquiesce to mere No?
You are going to think Yes, think Yes!

Keep on coming, keep on walking,
you can make it all the way
from St. Henry to the high school
in Holland, Indiana. I see you coming
from afar, I am here waiting for you
behind the desk. If nobody else will
wait for you as a teacher, I will.
I know how smart you are.
I have seen you multiply those
numbers on demand. I have heard
you speak both German and English.
I know what you can do, I believe
in you, you can make it, you will
do it, yes you will. You have not
yet had the terrible car crash
in the night that crippled your knee
and led to the wrong blood
being given to you in the hospital.
You can move ahead on your own.

No, no, you are going to do this,
you are going to make it all the way.
You are going to do whatever you
want and know you can do, you
are going to read, speak, figure,
you are going to move ahead,
you are not going to be left behind.

You are going to speak with the best
of them, even though you have
something of a German accent.

I am proud of you for doing this

on your own, for not accepting No,
for thinking Yes, for striking out
on your own no matter the distance,
no matter the obstacles. Yes,
I wait for you behind this desk.
Your books, paper, and pen wait
on the desk for you to arrive.

You are not wrong to disobey
your father. I will write him
a note that will make him proud.
He will come to understand
how badly you want to learn.
My father, I stand behind you.

Falling Shadows

Their shadows fell on me
as I listened to them
speak in German

and I followed them
as they walked
toward the end

of their lives
and I looked up
to see where they

were going and my
shadow falls on you
as you read my words

or hear me say them
so their sounds
fall in your ears

like shadows
of a world
I leave you.

Virgil in Hill Country

Virgil, Virgil,
how could I know
I'd find you here,

where I was born
and grew up, my
parents the same

and theirs too, after
some of us came over
across the big water

from where I was
sure you had stayed
over the centuries.

Virgil, Virgil,
not too many farmers
raise sheep in these hills,

but here you are,
shepherd as songster
singing your love

of the lady and the land
I thought were mine
to explore and praise.

I see you squinting up
at a fox squirrel cutting
in a shagbark hickory

in the woods
where I hunted
with my father.

Virgil, Virgil,
maybe you are
my daddy after all.

One small hill
can inspire a song
that travels the world.

Young Hunter's Prayer

How could I have known
as a boy that when
I hunted in the woods
I was learning to pray?

My father taught me
to circle a tree
in total silence
not disturbing a leaf

on the ground beneath.
Look up, he said,
and open your eyes.
Wait for any movement.

Stay completely still
for what seems forever.
Close your eyes, then
let them open again.

See with your ears,
speak with your eyes.
Lay down your gun.
The leaves will whisper.

Woods Time

for Nancy Lord

Once you have entered
into woods time, you carry it
with you forever, even if you
do not always live in it. Once
you move into woods time you
remain buoyant and float along.
Your senses intensify, what
is beyond enters into you,
and you extend outward into it.

Each bird song becomes individual
and speaks in such a way that enables
you to name the artist who sings.
Each tree presents a unique shape
of leaf, color and texture of bark
and gives a fruit to taste and chew.

Every creature that lives in the domain
of branch and bole and hole in trunk
and nest of leaves wears a different
kind of coat and color and speaks
in a particular cry or bark
and moves in its way up or down
and from one tree to another
with an economy of energy
and crawl or lurch or leap
that comes as a revelation
and remains as a marvel
in your full-color memory.

In woods time, no clocks
but the sun and the moon
and the stars and their seconds
and minutes and hours
and eons tell the story

of what every day can bring.
Breezes and winds tell
their stories by how they
make leaves turn, branches
clack, and whole trunks crash
down stripping other branches,
settling with a thump to an earth
of many-layered leaves.

This is the language my father
gave to me when I was nine
as he led me into the woods.
I speak in this tongue
I would have you pass on
to your son and daughter,
this language of the time
outside of time, of coming
into the expanse of the woods,
time not so much measured
as it is savored and stored
so that it may be recalled
and relived over and over
and passed on to those
who come after us.

Orchards

Though he kept his own counsel
I was aware as a boy of my father's

sorrow over his inability to reproduce
a colony of fruit trees like those

that grew in his father's orchard.
He would intone his sad litany:

pears, apples, peaches, apricots.
My husbandry is no more

than mediocre, but the fruits
of my father's orchard blossom

in these lines I cultivate with his
love of earth, branch, and leaf.

Christmas Paper Mountain Drifts

We opened the living room doors,
closed for the rest of the winter,
and opened the hot air vents.

An evergreen tree appeared overnight
before the picture window overlooking
what was in the those years a rye field.

A loop of popcorn on a long string
wound around evergreen boughs
between hand-painted ornaments.

Cookies and candies baked
in the kitchen came to rest
on a coffee table along the wall.

Tangerines kept cool in the closet
by the northern front door, when
peeled, gave off a refreshing aroma.

On Christmas Eve we opened presents
wrapped in shiny green, red, and silver
paper stacked in piles beneath the tree.

All the colored paper fell in crumpled
wads all over the rug so that we trudged
in great drifts of holiday avalanche.

The higher the paper drifts rose,
the higher our level of excitement.
We reveled in holiday anarchy.

Why could we not stay lost in those
crinkly drifts of red, green, silver?
Why did we all have to clean up?

Who wanted to hike back down
the dangerous mountain and find
the dreary flat rug real again?

A Child's Intuition

Whether childhood was happy
or sad is not relevant, not to
the games or play or work
as the something felt that lay
beyond, yet was a part of all
that was and still is here, the sense
of something larger, pervasive,
in every nook and cranny
of woods and field and even
self, something distinctly real

but not always seen, a presence
from within that even as we
detect it in others,
we cast down our eyes
when it flashes like a fish
whose scales have caught
intense rays of the sun,

because to behold it directly
can cause blindness, this
perception of all that is holy,
sometimes sacred, sometimes
remote, sometimes so present
and vital and pure that to deny
it would be yet another death.

Fieldstone

He would come home late
in the afternoon from selling
insurance in the country
to farmers in German

the trunk loaded down
with fieldstone, irregular shapes,
mostly flat, different colors,
often tan, brown, yellow,

but some red, gray, white
streaks, in various
combinations, cool to
the touch from hiding

from the sun in the trunk.
It must have been sandstone,
quartz or feldspar,
part of the earth's surface

cracked off by expansion
and contraction, heaved up
in the spring and picked up
when the farmer plowed,

or found in the creek bed
or maybe stuck in a bank,
or just glowing in the sun
at the edge of a woods

where a tree came down
and the roots pulled up.
He knew how to dig and lay
them down level to the surface

of the lawn, set them in
as a walk to where the swing
was hung between the sugar
maple and the dying white oak,

beneath which he also laid them
for our feet to alight on when
we came back to solid earth.
He also laid a floor of them

where we placed the picnic table
under a sweet gum tree with stars
for leaves that burned red in the fall
and dropped spiked balls for fruit.

Our feet rested on them
as we sat at the table, said grace,
and ate the meals she brought
outside to enjoy in the breezes

that visited our hillside home.
He would never tell us where
he got them, where they came
from, as if to identify his source

would dry up his supply
and offend his benefactor,
ruin his well-kept secret,
his knowledge of how to

stay in touch with where
you came from, way out
in the faraway country
where you had to speak

an almost forgotten language,
where fieldstone was legal
tender available only to those
who had prepared themselves

to receive its blessing
as if it were the sacrament
that kept you in touch
with the core of the earth.

Boy Knives

If you could throw it
end over end so it
stuck in the ground,

making your buddy
stretch his legs wider
and wider till he collapsed

in a heap, your knife
brought you admirers
but also more challengers.

You could also use it
to whittle and chisel
the figure-four triggers

for rabbit traps
and gut and scrape
scales from sunfish

you caught in a creek,
pond, or lake and
brought home to fry.

If you knew how to slit
open rabbits you trapped
or squirrels you shot

so you could pull
and sling away the guts
and save the innards,

depositing the meat
in a bowl of salted
water that drew out

blood, you helped
the family by putting
meat on the table.

The long, gleaming
hunting knifes, worn
in a sheath, were more

prized than the ordinary
pocket knives which folded
but could also do the job.

The trick was to keep
your knife sharp, the blade
always honed and ready,

by rubbing and scraping it
across a sandstone sharpener
you spat onto, to reduce

friction. I have at my back
my father's pocket knife,
still sharp after decades,

resting on a bookshelf,
in this room where I
whittle my poems down

to the right size, give
them a sharp edge
so they cut and slice

into a subject, open
up feelings and let
them flow, slice

spirit and flesh
so what is left
quivers and hovers.

The Mayberry Café

A high-finned squad car
welcomes your arrival
on the town square.

That booth in the corner
is all for you
and the girl on your arm.

If you want
meatloaf and gravy
it's all yours, baby.

Ain't nothin' but
Elvis on the radio
and black and white on TV.

Whenever you come
back you are, once again,
King for a Day, oh yeah!

Casey's Question

We were all dressed up
as if to go to church,
but painfully underage,
my best friend and I,
so Casey had to ask:
"You boys are 21?"
We swore we were with
Senior Scout sincerity.

Right across Newton Street
from the great Romanesque
sandstone church our ancestors
built not long after they arrived
from Germany about a hundred
years before we were born,

well below the great tower
which dwarfed us all and housed
the mighty bells that tolled
whenever anybody died

we did our Saturday night
shuffle, our underage tap dance
on the hardwood floor,
our imitation of understated
adult swagger before we
had come of full age,
played our adult boy game
with a woman we liked.

Casey sold us a half pint
which I snuggled inside
my sport coat pocket.

It was Saturday night.
We knew where we were
going, to the Calumet Pavilion
suspended over the lake

on the outskirts of town where
live music pulsed and the wooden
dance floor throbbed over the water,

as our heads would the next
morning when our parents
called us to get up and go
to church with bloodshot eyes.

As we walked out the door,
old Casey smiled and said,
"Be careful, boys, but have
a good time." The time we had
was at least good that night
and others, but how much care
we took I cannot say for sure.

If Casey chuckled after
we went out the door,
she kept it to herself
and the God she knew
who lived across the street.

Decades later when I came
back to town to read my poems
in the same house that miraculously
became a bookstore, ready
to sign my books right
in the shadow of the tower
of the still majestic church,

the spirit of Casey must have
grinned somewhere beyond
waiting to ask me if I thought
I had finally come of age
enough to tell the whole truth.

White Knuckles

What comes back
is white knuckles
on the steering wheel

and us in the back
seat, silent, knowing
the way was dark

and the outcome
uncertain as she
sat next to him

trying to keep him
calm as he
struggled to keep

in control and not
give in to the fear
left over from

that time a car
came toward
him in the dark

with headlights
tunneling on the wrong
side of the road

and the crash
that always follows
you wherever you

go in the future
so that metal
exploding on metal

is a sound
your ears stay
always open to.

Monon Memories

In the dark we wound up and down
around the hills toward the small town

where the train stopped. Still in the dark,
I said goodbye to my parents for another

few months, boarded the train in Paoli,
with a suitcase full of fresh laundry

and partially underlined books, and lurched
north. Some towns like Mitchell and Orleans

I was awake for, others I dozed through,
even when I half heard their names,

as if being re-introduced to cousins
I'd met but didn't see often enough

to remember. And then I would be sitting
by myself in full daylight, wondering where

I was going, even though I knew the day's
destination. I wondered how a rolling

landscape I loved could turn so easily
into a monotony of windy flatness.

Would I ever wake up to where
I'd come from and what that means?

At a stop in Rensselaer, I knew it was
my place to get off. Aware that I was

the first to go to college since those
whose names I did not yet know

had come down the Ohio River
a long time ago, I lifted my suitcase

of books and clothes and started the long
walk back to the Catholic campus on the other

side of town. It never occurred to me to call
a cab, if there was a cab to call in a town

so small. Lugging the suitcase, I turned
in the right direction and put down one

foot at a time, just as they had done
when they stepped off the big boat

and began the long journey into the interior
which led to the walk I was taking.

110

The Beatles Cut

I'm sitting there in his chair
looking out the window
at traffic passing on Main Street.
Cloth over me all the way up
to my neck, his scissors going
snip, snip. Nothing on the radio,
just his voice working the air
slowly, as if to move it around,
shake things up a bit, entertain.
Barber as small town newscaster.
Others sitting there pretending
they aren't listening, but tuned in.

I'd been thinking about what
John Lennon said, that it
wasn't too smart to say they'd
become bigger than Jesus,
no matter what he meant.
Folks around here don't go
for that kind of talk, even
if they like a man's song
and the sound of his voice
with guitar, bass, and drum
wrapped all around it, harmonies
lifting it up and down, No, Sir!
Snip, snip go the scissors.

I admit my hair had grown
a bit longer, but that was happening
to all of us, war on the evening news,
draft coming closer and closer,
friends being sent over there
to that messy, scary jungle,
some coming back in bags.

"You hear about the guy from
Otwell?" he asks between snips.
Since I was away in college,
he knows I can't keep up
with every little detail of what
goes down in my hometown,
though we all talk a lot
and a few write letters.
Seems like the others
waiting their turn in their
chairs are listening maybe
a little too hard. But we all
like to hear good stories.

"Well," he continues, "that
Otwell boy let them hairs
grow longer and longer,
like he was fixin' to become
a rock singer, maybe a Beatle.
No telling how big he thought
he might one day become."

Snip, snip, scissors come
closer and closer, growing sharper
and sharper. "So a buncha his
friends wrestled him down
to the ground, held his arms
behind his back. Someone else
got out his mama's scissors
borrowed from the sewing kit
and went snip, snip, snip.
No more rock singer, no more
Beatle boots, no more getting
bigger than Jesus ever was."

Everybody in that place
looking at me real hard now,
grins licking at their faces,
my hair feeling shorter
and shorter, like back
in the days of the flattop.
White sidewalls upside the head
is what I start to feel I will
carry back to college.

The Barbed Wire Tattoo

for Barb and Chuck Stevenson

Four of us on the Heichelbech's
Tavern softball team tore off
to the Sunday races in Salem,

top down. I siphoned a six pack
between Jasper and Haysville,
six miles. Excellent mileage.

You could say I was primed,
but not for anything good.
After we arrived at the track,

we peeled off our T-shirts,
rarin' to go. Don't know
how it started, maybe flammable

beer fumes ignited, but soon
a fight erupted and I found
myself right in it. I was punching

at somebody through a barbed wire
fence and he was punching back.
Don't know if I hit him, but barbed

wire blades cut three white stripes
on the inside of my upper left arm
where nobody but an undertaker

will ever look. Let's call this
a memento of youthful excess,
a gratuitous white tattoo that

never went away. Within minutes
after the fence slashed me bloody,
my enemy and I laid our arms

around one another's shoulders.
I don't recall what song we may
have sung together, but it must

have had something to do with peace
and love before that combination
for the Beatles hit number one.

War was percolating, peace was not yet
ready to blow in the wind, and the white
tattoo will descend with me into the earth.

Dogwoods and Redbuds for Rita

We come driving south
into the hills in the rain,
to settle you into the earth.

Dogwoods and redbuds for Rita,
white and pink in the woods
turning green with new leaves
unfurling everywhere sheath wet.

You suffered, for so many years,
the agony of trying to speak

we must send you off
with a gift of very few words,
our father's baby sister,
last of ten children,
released at eighty-six.

We give you dogwoods and redbuds
in blossom and green leaves opening.
We give you gentle rain falling
on the rolling hills we love.

We give you dogwoods and redbuds
and rain falling on new leaves, Rita.

We form a choir of relatives
and sing thee to thy rest,

and sing thee to thy rest.

The Old America

They came out of the old America.
He knew the sounds of the saloon
above which he was born,
the rise of raucous laughter
lifted by barley and hops,
the sight of late afternoon
sun slanting through the window
coming to lie down on floorboards.
She knew the beat of fresh milk
squeezed from the swollen teat
splashing against the bottom
and sides of a granite bucket,
the high and lonesome wail
of her daddy's pure tenor
as he strummed the mandolin
higher and higher to get
the rise of the winter wind
to come inside the farmhouse.
He knew the scream of his
father's circular saw ripping
into the great white oak logs
waiting to be cut into lumber.
Her legs knew how to take
her down into the little woods
at the far end of the pasture
where she stirred the corn mash
before turning around and skipping
through the weeds as if she had never
done anything wrong and just
wanted to play with her rag doll.
He would grow up to play fiddle
at barn dances, to feel the flow
of notes rising out of the scrape
of his bow across the strings.

She would move into the dance
that took over her ready feet
and one night led into his
waiting arms. My parents came
out of a tiny Civil War village
and a small hand-me-down farm
and a country that is still part
of me but dies a little bit
every day as the sun climbs
up in the East and rolls down
in the West as I hold on to
the voices that were theirs.

2 *A Blank Piece of Paper*

A Blank Piece of Paper

Between dark hills
somewhere in this land
a boy sits at a table
next to a dim light.

He stares at a blank
piece of paper,
holding a pen
filled with enough ink
to tell a good story.

What the boy can't yet
tell is where he began
and where he will end

but even though he is
somewhere not quite
in the middle of
whatever story is his

he knows the time
has come for him
to let the ink flow.

He can feel the first
line poise on the
tip of his pen.

Let the story begin
wherever the tip
of his pen touches
the piece of paper.

Even though our boy
will spend several
lifetimes trying to
move his pen
toward the ending
of the story,

each time he moves
halfway there, more ink
will come into the pen.

Though he will never
tell the whole story,

in the telling
of every new half
of the story
always left to tell

the boy will
make his life
twice as large

and ours as
full as it
can become.

Brother Antoninus / William Everson at Notre Dame, 1965

for John Groppe

A man on stage in a white robe
with a cincture around his waist
and sandals on his feet pulls
a black electric cord attached
to a microphone, making it
wriggle like a snake perhaps
to snare our attention.

We are gathered in the library
of a Catholic university. He is Dominican,
not forever, and Beat; but the names
of orders and literary movements
did not bring me here to take notes.

It is the mid-1960s. He is a famous poet.
A neophyte in graduate school, I want
this holy man's words to enter
my blood and expand my psyche.

I want to learn outside textbooks
how to hear the sounds and silences
of one man's language and witness
a living example of how spirit
can come to dwell in the word.

I feel the poet's words pass
between us and pull us together
in a shared ritual that binds
us into a catacomb community.

He helps me begin to see
that words charged with spirit
go deepest, ripen longest,
break through the surface

and when seasons and planets align
rise like waterbirds soaring
toward home in earliest light,
crying out their heartsong
above waters turning below.

A Hoosier Song of Walt Whitman

It was like the pounding,
recurring roar of the sea
I had never seen or heard
deep in my Midwestern youth,
but could remember from
some other life. That slow,
rhythmic song of a boy
who stepped forth on a fish-
shaped island and watched
lamb fetuses push forth
from the womb, lilac leaves
sway in salt breeze,
and the town drunk stagger
past the schoolmistress
on his way home from a binge.
That spiraling song carried
all the way to my inland
island in the hills
of southern Indiana
and hummed in my ears
like the sea in a shell
mysteriously deposited
a thousand miles away.
And when I went forth from
my Indiana island and landed
by accident on that child's
Paumanok, I listened to
the surf pound the shore,
turned inland, and caught
the voice of the boy
who stepped forth to sing
for the man who now looks back
the songs of the people
whose breath fills his lungs.

Basho's Journey

If Basho journeyed
to the far north,
I'll go into

the hills of
the south where
spirit can disappear.

When a place
holds your past,
go down into it.

What you explore
may be dark, but
you'll find eyes.

With vision,
we can go
beyond any here.

The Family Farm: For Wendell Berry

1

Barefoot, carefree, and happy,
I help a cousin bring in the cows
from the pasture on the farm
where my mother grew up.
We sidestep the dung balls
beetles rolled from platters.
In the milking room of the barn,
no electric rubber mouth sucks
and pulses milk into a glass tube;
mostly the hands of cousins,
wrapped around the teats,
squeeze and squirt milk
into metal pails in a soft,
regular beat. My happy
hand, still warm, tingles.

2

In the barn I climb
the round wooden rungs
to the loft and swing wide
on a thick rope, let loose,
and thump onto straw stacked
in bales exhaling the smell
of grain and hay fields
ripening in summer sun.

3

In the smokehouse, hams
hang to cure. In a crock
in the corner, blackberry juice
ferments; in the back room,
the inner sanctuary, moonshine

gathers potency in glass jugs.
Up in the attic huddles
a Victrola with a crank
and a bulldog icon
poised to bark and croon.

4

Beside the chicken house
two coonhounds lie angled
away from one another,
dreaming of one more night
in the woods a pasture away.
Their whiskers twitch
as they breathe in and out.

5

In a shabby shed where
he is sometimes left
during the day stands
the old work horse, Charlie,
now replaced by a tractor
with cleated metal wheels.
My hand fits perfectly
in the space between
his fading eyes and rests
on his neck when
he lowers his head.

6

Not far from the ancient
sugar maple shading the well
where we draw cold water
and sip it from a tin cup
chained to the pump
is the spot where men in overalls
and jackets gathered in the cold

to slaughter pigs. One of them
was my grandfather. He died
young, leaving a widow
with six children. The eldest,
my godfather, was twelve.
My mother was six.

7

Neighbors and relatives came
to help with the hay, the combining,
the harvesting of corn, the butchering.
One of the daughters slipped down
the path in the pasture to the woods
to stir the corn mash once a day.
This was my mother's secret.
A long pipeline flowed with
White Lightning from the hills
of Dubois County to Louisville.
Revenoors were anathema.

8

Dancing in the barn, skating on the pond,
swimming in the White River, squirrel
and rabbit in the skillet, with dark gravy,
and sometimes quail in the oven.
Fried catfish, bluegills, frog legs;
pork and blood sausage, ham, bacon,
chicken, some Sundays a roast,
always vegetables from the garden.
Hominy and cornmush. Persimmons,
pawpaws, blackberries, wild grapes,
walnuts, hickory nuts, pecans, mushrooms.
Singing in the parlor. Work, hard work,
in the house, the barnyard, the barn,
the field. Six children walking
to school, three miles each way.
The father's mandolin stayed slack
in the closet, his tenor hushed, as his
widow and six children pulled through.
Poor, yes poor, but rich in the ways
of woods and field and crops
and wise about animals,
like the Coulters and the Feltners,
the Beechums and the Branches,
the Wheelers and the Catletts,
families who farmed the land
near Port William, Kentucky.

9

In the barber shop in the town
in the hills of southern Indiana,
the men come and go
talking of Joe DiMaggio.
Mr. Daschle of Jasper, Indiana,
kin to Jayber Crow of Port William,
snip snips at their hair and listens,

as my father and I do, too.
Many of the men moved
from the farm to the town
and worked in wood factories
until they retired and have come
to roost in the barber shop,
to crow about crops and squirrels
and how it's all going downhill.
My father, who grew up
in the country, moved to town
to work in a chair factory,
and now sells insurance,
talks to them in German.
They all shake their heads.
The oldest of them rise,
shakily, like Old Jack Beechum,
of the Port William membership,
and shuffle with their canes to perch
on the bench outside the courthouse
like hawks to watch cars circle.

10

Decades pass, I leave
town for a job far away,
my father dies, and we
return home often to visit.
We drive from Jasper
with my mother to visit
my godfather, retired farmer
and country road supervisor
who once put me on a road crew.
His oldest sons, now fathers,
pull up, call us "city slickers"
as they pump and sip water, throw
some on the dry grass, lurch off
on a tractor or spin rocks
with a pickup, rushing back

to work in the field. No time
to talk to folks like us, except
to grouse about the plight of the farmer.
Their aunt, my mother, keeps
the peace by keeping quiet.
The ghost of Hannah Coulter,
wise and enduring mother
of Kentucky, abides at her side.

11

Catalpa beans hang
dry as dead bones.
An old tractor stands
in the shed like
a sagging work horse
put out to pasture.
The hollyhocks and mums
no longer come up strong.
The silo wears stains
up and down its ribs,
the barn door
no longer closes,
and the coon hounds
have fallen asleep
forever beneath
the old walnut tree.

12

Someone with a name
I do not know leases
the family land to farm it.
I have to ask a favorite cousin
which of his older retired brothers
still lives in the farmhouse,
disconnected from the land.

13

Burley Coulter, wily woodsman
and able farmhand who left for days
to hunt in Wendell Berry's woods,
is dead and won't return in flesh.
May his wild spirit roam forever
on the ridges and in the hollows,
descending to speak only to those
who know where to look and listen.

The Campfire Poets

Coming down a back road,
I saw a campfire in the woods.

Tired, I wandered over,
slipped off my backpack,

looked down at a man and woman
whose eyes burned like coal.

He was fleshy, had a bushy gray beard;
she was petite, bursting with dark energy.

He said he was the poet of the body and soul
and all people; she said she wrote letters

to a world that never wrote back.
They moved a bit apart, he motioned

me to sit down between them,
and I knew I'd found eternity

off the side of a back road
in the hill country woods.

Emily Dickinson's Song

Sing me a song, Emily,
I said, and she laid one
on me like I never heard.

At once I tumbled head
over heels into the dark
that was somewhere inside

and hit millions of worlds
I never knew existed
and my eyes went out

and then somewhere else
I woke up and saw
that I had come into

a searing light that
turned everything in view
into x-ray versions

of the objects that were
like shadows in a cave
where Plato lived.

Then I looked up
and Emily sat smiling
in her white dress.

Moving in with Emily

I moved in with Emily
because we both like

to dwell in possibility.
Man, what a ride it was!

Sometimes I couldn't tell
if the horse's head was pointed

toward heaven or hell but
I wasn't about to jump off.

We generated so much heat
by the way we wrote our poems

we didn't burn a lot of wood.
For her, everything always

came out red-hot, but I took
a bit longer to get it going.

Mornings we woke up tired
from so much creative activity.

The doctor said we should
take it easy once in a while,

but Emily just grinned and said,
The soul selects her own society.

Now that she's gone and I read
her poems, it's hard to believe

I could have been there with her
when lighting struck the house.

Emily Dickinson's Travels

Never left home, they said,
but she traveled beyond
and deep within where internal
difference inheres. Her soul selected

her own society, she knew one
need not be a large chamber
to be haunted. She rode that
certain slant of light which

flashes us into worlds
that science can't measure.
She knew this world is not
conclusion and explored another,

took the route of evanescence
and soared on whirring wings
of hummingbirds that delivered
her to a Tunis in the mind.

She had no time to stop for death
because she was always descending
into and beyond herself to taste a liquor
never brewed, telling all the dark

truth but telling it slant, writing
letters to a world that never
wrote back, staring into mysteries
that pervade wells, growing

accustomed to the dark. She
kept the Sabbath by looking
at creatures outside her self,
ecstatic to hear an oriole sing

but unsure of the source of
the song or what it signified,
certain only that success
was counted sweetest by those

who never succeed. She lived
and died for beauty but was
reborn into the glorious gift
of being able to make a prairie

with just one clover and one
single solitary but potent bee.
She dwelt eternally in possibility.
Her carriage held Immortality.

Song for Gabriela Mistral

You are deep and dark
Gabriela Mistral, Lucila
Godoy de Alcayagua,

but your poems give off
a light that comes from
the depths of the earth

and somewhere beyond.
Your lines are coiled tight
like the heart of the rose,

elemental, mysterious
like the folds
at the center

of all that is female.
Daughter eternal,
you come of the hills.

You carry the place
of your birth
wherever you wander,

ever connected to
a primal source.
You always go back,

in passionate love
with water, air, wind,
the capricious colors

of plants, their dance
with one another and you
on the Chilean earth.

You are a vessel
of blessings poured full,
bearer of dark red wine

for us to sip,
savor on the lips,
taste on the tongue.

Basho's Waters

No matter how far
he journeyed
into the interior

Basho always knew
how to arrive
where water gathers.

He listened to
frogs plunge into
the sound of water.

He watched the river
sweep a hot day
away into the sea.

He saw the camellia
pour rain water
when it leaned,

the windblown banana
tree pour rain drops
into a bucket.

He watched tides
slide in and foam
in autumn full moon.

Autumn rain made
mountains beyond
beautiful to the eye.

Hearing dew drops
drip, he wished
to wash the world.

He walked round
and round a pond
in harvest moon.

Moving, he cast
his shadow like
a divining rod

to find and tap
the ancient well
from which

he allowed
his readers
to drink deep.

Walt Whitman on the South Shore

for David Steinberg

When Walt Whitman stood as a boy
on the South Shore of the Island
on which he was born, he listened

to the midnight roar of the waves
crash onto the sand and ebb
back out toward the depths.

Between the crash and the ebb,
he heard the sad notes of a bird
lamenting its loss of a mate.

From the moment of this rebirth,
he knew his calling was to sing of loss
but also light, sadness but also joy.

He learned that when you accept
the call, there is no going back
to the boy you once were before

you took on your lifelong mission:
the pain and the tumult, yes, but also
the sweet taste of singing for all.

Looking for Walt Whitman on Campus

If you want me again look
for me under your boot-soles. "Song of Myself"

I went looking for you, Walt,
all over campus after we read
your Paumanok poems.

Not far from where I once sat
at the top of stone steps reciting
"Give Me the Splendid Silent Sun,"
I saw boot prints in the mulch
of flower beds in the formal garden
beside the administration building.

In the woods along
the arboretum walk, I picked up
those tracks again and swear
I could hear your bardic voice
trill and catalog the names
of American hardwoods
as if you were reciting
the names of the saints.

In the recesses of the library
stacks I spied your gray-bearded
presence peering into volumes
of experimental poems from
the heart of the continent.

Walking down the hall
where one class door was ajar
I saw a familiar colleague
with his mouth wide open
but heard you declaring
to his wide-eyed students
our independence from
Old World hegemony

and insisting we must open
our doors more to immigrants
and those the system despises
and let our instincts speak
more fully without check.

I was afraid, Walt, what kind
of revolution you might foment.
I opened my mouth to issue
a warning to the young about
the potential danger of your
influence, but all that came out
were words I recognized as yours,

I bequeath myself to the dirt
to grow from the grass I love,

and I knew that wherever I stepped
on this campus and your Island
I would always be touching you.

Mockingbird Memory

After we finish talking about
Whitman's poem of childhood
memory based on the story
of mockingbird lovers separated
by death on the shores of this Island
where the boy absorbs the tale
of love lost and is reborn
as the poet who now looks back
at the scene from his youth
and sees the mystical interplay
between life and death and finds
his mission is to put together
a musical arrangement of words
that survive the onslaught of time

there is a pause and I hear
a sliding song issuing from
the old black walnut tree
where I have seen generations
of the songbird with the white
wing bars and the musical
shuttle in their throats
near the corner of Humanities
Hall where we sit and reflect.

I ask if anyone knows
what that sound is and none
of the natives of Paumanok's
suburbs recognizes it as
the music of the mockingbird

and I am brought back to memories
of walnut trees in southern Indiana
where as a boy I picked up the lobed
green fruits that turned dark brown
and carried them home in a burlap
bag slung over my shoulder.

The lyric of mimicry sliding
from the tree outside the hall
on this quiet day tallies with
the tale of the Long Island poet's
revisitation of the mystical play

of moonlight and shadow on the shores
that he loved where he found the voice
that sings his poems of loss and rebirth

and I awaken as the boy I was
in the hills of southern Indiana
with a burlap bag of walnuts
over my shoulder and at the same
time remain the man that I have
become on Whitman's Long Island
a thousand miles away from the hills
where I haunted the woods and fields.

Now I see that song in trees
and in poems carries us beyond
where we come from and where
we go and takes us well beyond
ourselves and this world where
we live until we depart as spirit

that will one day shine back down
on a bird singing its song woven
from the songs of others while young
people sit at their desks yearning
to find the voice that carries them
beyond where they now are to
what they hope they shall become.

Prayer to Walt Whitman at Ground Zero

Come back, Walt Whitman, we need you now in the
hour of our grief.
Come back, Camerado, wind your way back to Ground
Zero where you belong.
Wrap your arm around the shoulder of a fireman who
lost his best friend,
tell the policemen how brave their brothers were at the
moment of collapse,
rub your fingers between the ears of the dog that has
sniffed hour after hour for the smell of human
flesh,
stand at attention when workers find in the rubble the
body of a brother,
amble over to the Armory and say a word to long lines
of those who have pictures of their loved ones
pinned to their chests,
tell the husband how beautiful and good his missing
wife is,
tell the wife how courageous her husband was to help
his colleagues,
promise the sister you will hunt with her for her lost
brother just as you hunted for brother George at
Fredericksburg,
hold steady the mother and father who lost their son
weeks before he was to marry,
hug the student from Queens who, after her class in the
suburbs rode your word-ferry across time and
space, sobbed to her teacher they had found the
body of her firefighter-fiancé,
comfort the family of the Brooklyn student who came
to this country from Syria for asylum and will
now return home only in spirit,

guide to sanctuary the refugees who, white ash and
ghostly powder disfiguring their faces, hobbled
across the Brooklyn bridge toward your old
haunts,
you who know so well the underbelly of this city and
the pulse of the people.

Come back to smoking Manahatta, Father Walt, where
you walked the streets with immigrants from
many lands
and rode the omnibus and listened to the Italian opera
and the American folk song
and applauded the singer and rode the ferry back to
Brooklyn,
convince us the lilac will blossom again and release its
fragrance into the air,
help us believe the mockingbird will trill and caper, the
hermit thrush sing, and the children smile, shout
and play in the parks again without looking up.

Come back and implore the wounded moon to pour her
mysterious ministrations on us,
petition the splendid silent sun to come out and shine
long while wounds heal,
teach us a language that rises into prayer as we lift one
another,
help us not to fear our grief as we commemorate the
thousands lost,
show our leaders how to be judicious and strong,
compassionate and unflinching,
look over us as we read the poem-prayers that inform
our resolve to become larger than before, open-
hearted, strong, wise, patient,
keep waiting for us in the grass that grows beneath our
boot-soles.

Blueberries and Buttermilk: For William Stafford

William Stafford Memorial Tribute,
Walt Whitman Birthplace, May Day, 1994

"This place is a poem,"
began the poet who is
the poet's son, as he stood
with his back to the hearth
at which Quaker Louisa simmered
food for the boy who became
the poet after Emerson
brought him to a boil.

On the mantel painted the color
of blueberries mixed with buttermilk
stood two bright paintings
by his sister illustrating
two framed poems by his father.

"The hand-forged nails,"
he explained, "the bubbled
glass panes, the books
propping the window open,
the lilac blooming beyond,
the sun shining through."

My wife at my side, my son
and daughter at my back,
I thought of the rough carpenter
father for whom it could
not have been easy to have
a son who became a poet.

As I listened to this son's measured,
reassuring words, I thought it
could not be easy to become
and remain a poet if you are
the son of even a loving father
who is such a beloved poet.

We sat in Louisa's kitchen
like an extended family
of friends gathered for one
last meal and listened
with bowed heads to the story
of the last few days:

writing new poems, going
on old walks, cutting grass,
taking a nap, stepping into the study,
being called to the kitchen
when the blender exploded.

After tinkering with the machine,
as he loved to do with words,
he said, "Better get a new
spatula," and slumped.

We sat in Sunday afternoon
shadows that thickened as
we listened to the strong poems
of the last days delivered
in the voice of the son which
caught the tone of the father.
There were moments when son
flickered into father but then
stepped forth as father of his
own family and shaper of his
own words as late poems settled.

Then we rose in Quaker fashion,
when the spirit so moved us,
to read a favorite poem.

When my call came, I read
a poem he wrote for a book
of writings by poets I once
put together in honor of
an earlier poet from Roslyn,
"At Bryant's Grave." I heard
my voice say, "Translated by
the years, he abides with
the sound of his words."

Leaves United for Etheridge Knight at Crown Hill Cemetery

Etheridge, the dry brown
oak, maple, and beech leaves

have gathered around to touch
your flat gray tombstone

and testify with the other elements
that you a free singer still be!

Rumi for Breakfast

I am in a hospital cafeteria
eating breakfast, looking out
on a garden of pink roses,

green lily and pachysandra.
My mouth is eating scrambled
eggs and fruit and sipping tea.

My mind and spirit are reading
Rumi's poems about living
in two worlds, the outer and inner,

about being in one place
and another at the same time.
As I take sip after sip

of this spirit, I feel
healthier and healthier.
Rumi, what a doctor!

Rumi's Mysterious Rays

Rumi, you medieval devil,
how have you done it?

Copies of your poems
are everywhere

in this late empire
of plastic and quick fry.

People carry your
visions into dream

or turn on a dim lamp
to ingest you before dawn.

Lovers read your ecstatic
inward lines to one another,

inhale uncontrollably,
and sigh slowly.

But nothing is easy
or hard in your world,

you who go down or up
with speed and insight

that give off mysterious
rays of illumination.

The Mad Underliner

after reading Rachel Peden's Rural Free

Somewhere in this house
hides a mad underliner.
He's way too shrewd
to be caught in the act,
knows he must conceal
his compulsion from others.

When the house is quiet,
after the children have fallen
into the arms of sleep
and his wife turns off
her light and sinks
with heavy lids down
into the dark warm waters,
the mad underliner
comes fully alive.

Now it's just the man
and the book he craves
left alone in the glow
of one reading lamp to
do whatever they want.

She allows him to open
her where they last stopped.
He feels for the page last
crimped in her top corner.
Out comes his ready pen.
Dark flows the ink, like
a wet tattoo that wants
to spread all over her
most beautiful body
of words, sentences,
paragraphs, chapters.

Silent is the tick of the clock.
Gone are the rules of the world.
The mad underliner finds
himself to be where he
has always longed to be:
alone, unwatched, ungoverned,
with the most gorgeous
book he has ever found,
free to underline every
luminous word his eyes
deliver into his heart.

Caveat Emptor

Do not attempt to operate heavy machinery
after hearing and absorbing this poem.

Do not imbibe this poem
if you have liver problems.

This poem could make you see funny
and talk a very strange language.

Share this poem only with someone
with whom you have been intimate.

If you ingest this poem whole,
you may be arrested for substance abuse.

If you are afraid of being stoned forever,
smoke this poem but don't dare inhale.

If you want to act presidential,
this poem is definitely not for you.

The people who bring you this poem do not
accept responsibility for what it does to you.

If this poem keeps you aroused for over
four hours, call the poetry police at once.

All you have to do to turn them into flower
children who love you is read them the best line.

This is your lucky day: the people who wrote
this poem invite you to spend the night for free.

Strike up the band, turn down the lights,
this poem will dance with you cheek to cheek.

Mulberry Blues

Mulberry, mulberry,
why you want
to do this to me?

Since I was a boy,
I sought you out,
loved your shape
and the taste
of your fruit
which I pressed
against my palate
to savor its juice.

Mulberry, mulberry,
why you do me wrong?
Why you do this despite
my devotion decades long?

Over the years
I found you
deep in the Midwest
and along the streets
and cracked sidewalks
of faraway Long Island.

Wherever and whenever
you were ripe, I came
and stood in your shadows,
not caring if others saw me
devour your fruits after
they drooped and dropped
into my outstretched hands
like gifts from the gods.

Mulberry, mulberry
how you justify laying
on me these bitter blues?

Doctors now tell me
that among all the trees
I love, you do me
the most damage.

When your pollen hangs
in the air I inhale,
you tickle my throat,
make me swallow hard,
insinuate your spell
into my vocal chords,
make them stop
vibrating the right way,
and rob me of the voice
to sing my love of you.

I did not know people
make of your bark fine
paper on which to write.
If only I had known,
I would have etched
on your dark skin
a love song for the ages.

Mulberry, mulberry,
I come to scratch this
heartsong into the flesh
of your precious bark.

I can't stop these feet
from finding your
presence to bow before,
no matter what you do,

even as you give me
a bad dose of the blues
that deepens my voice
until it surrenders all hues
and I cannot say adieu.

A Word Story

When the word comes
you better open the door.
Don't worry what color
it wears or what language
it speaks. When the word
comes knocking, open
the door. Keep the word
to yourself, if you must,
or share it with others.

Open your house
and gardens for a word
party, if you like,
and introduce the word
to friends and family.
You could even become
the word laureate for
your neighborhood.
The pay is poor but
the benefits are many.

If you can put words
together in the right way
and say them with
a rhythm that can't help
but sing, people will ask
you to come into their
houses to make a word
party. A publisher might
slip out of the woods
and offer to put your
words between covers
and your name above
the front door where
it will sit inviting others
inside your word house.

Yes, open those doors,
ladies and gentlemen.
Let the word come
in and also go forth:
the time of the word
has come. Put the word
on tablets if you like,
as well as on paper. Carve
the word in stone. Inject
the word into a song
and sing your lyric
to the world. Be old-
fashioned and sit around
the fire and tell stories
made of old words
combined with the new.

Words transcend political
parties and cross lines
between countries.
Words can peacefully
sneak into other languages
and stop long wars.
Some words know how
to kiss you in the right
place when you're
not looking. Others are
adept at sneaking up
behind you and making
you smile when you
are feeling low.

Some word friends go
so far as to say that
for millennia the word
has been man and woman's
best friend. So if you feel
a word breathing at the door,

open it and put out a bowl
of fresh milk. You may
make a loyal friend who
will stay at your side
the rest of your life.

3 Practically with the Band

The Fiddler

Once taking a walk
beneath trees in Lockerbie Square,
near the James Whitcomb Riley House,
I heard the sound of a fiddle.

I looked around and up
and saw an opening of sky
and heard the sounds
of a dance in an old barn.

My father, a teenager,
was playing the fiddle
and friends and relatives
were clapping and dancing

and horses were tied
outside the barn and there
was beer in dark bottles
and white lightning

in a clear jug that made
the rounds and rose to
many lips and my father's
bow scraped across the strings.

As the rhythm of his tune
raced faster and faster
women's dresses whirled
and men's feet stamped

and there was one *yee-haw*
after another on a Saturday
night as the grin on my father's
face stretched wide as the sky.

Goodnight, Irene

Somewhere in my childhood
I hear Leadbelly singing

"Goodnight, Irene," the melody
arising as if out of the earth,

carried by many voices
reduced to one that has

been chosen to sing for all.
Then it is joined by a woman's

voice, one I recognize instantly,
welling up right next to me.

This is my mother, singing
along, as if no choice were

involved, giving herself
to a sound that claimed her

and spoke through her,
as if she wrote it herself.

And so I say goodnight
to Irene, a beautiful woman

whose spirit is reduced to
the sweet sound of a vowel

and "n" that rhyme with keen
and joins with a drawn-out dream

that tugs me to a land
where sleep is enlarged

and extended by the voices
of men and women who give

themselves to an ancient song
that lifts and carries us beyond

ourselves and turns us into
pure sound that wings higher

and soars away to where
blue sky and water are one.

I'm Practically with the Band

for the Spud Puppies, with thanks to Chuck Stevenson

Oh, yeah, I'm practically with the band.
They need dobro, dobro is what I play.
They need piano, I can honkey-tonk.
They need mandolin, I pick it clean.
Clawhammer banjo? I can bum-ditty strum.
Lead guitar? I can wail it or understate it.
They need base, I pluck it subterranean.
Fiddle, you bet: slow slurs, racy runs.
They need accordion, I squeeze with the best.
They need a steady beat, I pound the drum.
They need harmony vocals, harmony I sing.
They need lead vocal, I can sing that, too.

Now I ain't sayin' where or how long
I been playin' any or all o' these,
but I'm practically with the band.
I know all their songs so well
sometimes I think I wrote 'em myself.
I own every one of their CDs
and some they won't dare release.
I write and recite a mean original poem
to give the boys in the band a break,
and if they're one song short
I crank out a good one, 1, 2, 3.

Now I'm normally a pretty shy guy,
but if the band needs somebody
to swing a sweetheart onto the dance floor
who can shake it like a knockout mixed drink
and make the crowd go wild and wooly,
well, just maybe I could do that, too.

Yeah, I'm practically with the band.
You can color me bluegrass or newgrass,
you can croon me country or rockabilly me,

you can rock and roll me, slide and bottleneck me,
you can murder me with an old mountain ballad,
you can love me tender or hard as you like,
you can lonesome me ever so lowdown and blue.

You all know we are the folk, we are the music.
We are every note, every word of every song.
Oh, yeah, we're all practically with the band.

Woody Guthrie's Guitar Machine

This machine kills fascists.

His guitar machine
killed fascists and other
manglers of spirit

and his words
sung to the machine
killed even more

agents of injustice
than the authorities
could ever know

and now his songs
are anthems we sing
to revive our souls

and a land in need
of more machines
that kill to save.

Oklahoma Poem Beginning and Ending with Woody Guthrie

for Jeanetta Calhoun Mish

1. Oklahoma Hills

Coming over every hill
in Eastern Oklahoma you
hear a Woody Guthrie song.

2. Outside Wewoka

The spirits of our friend's
grandparents sit waving
on a hill of their farm.

3. Hometown Lunch

Fried catfish and okra
lie down on the plate
and make Okie whoopy.

4. Her Sister

Blue eyes dart here and there
as tongue turns for words to say
she loves being back together.

5. Seminole Museum Wewoka

Little neighbor Louis has
grown up into a big cousin
who directs education.

6. Open Wewoka Eye

Everywhere you look
in Wewoka a poem
waits to pop out.

7. Little Niagra, Sulphur

Like her ancestors, we stick
our feet in cold sulphur waters
to wash our worries away.

8. Okemah Vision

I see everywhere little boy
Woody Guthrie ride his pony
among the Indian nations.

Listening to Live Music

When I listen to music live, I'm there and not there. Sometimes I enter all the way into a song and am completely gone in the songwriter's vision, lifted up and pushed along by the guitar's rhythmic strum. Sometimes I stay gone after the song ends and do not want to return to where I was before it began. Sometimes, in the middle of a concert, I start to write my own song or poem, as I am doing right now. There are times when I can't tell the difference between writing a poem and a song and don't know if I'm Walt Whitman or Woody Guthrie. You have to admit that's an attractive sort of confusion. What I really like is when I'm so gone into the poem or song or whatever it is I've written that my wife has to tap me on the head to make me realize that she's neither Joan Baez nor Emily Dickinson. "Well, Mr. Zimmerman, welcome back to reality," she says unkindly. "Or is it Mr. Dylan I'm talking to today? Welcome back home, Bobbie!"

Song for Bobbie D

Hey, hey, Bobbie D,
I wrote you a poem
about a Midwestern boy
who arrived and showed 'em

how to take an old folk song
and turn it into something new
that comes from all times and places
and speaks to both me and you.

Here's to the singers
and songwriters who
came to the New York Village
to play and carouse and do

what musicians love to do:
make music, drink wine, read
poems that tell weird stories
about human foibles and greed.

Hey, hey, Bobbie D,
here's to you and Joan
and Dave and Robert Johnson
and Odetta and your own

favorite hobo, old Woody G.
Here's to the red-hot words
you struck into flame as you
strummed the ancient chords

and here's to the visions
and revisions that carried
you through many a rebirth
as you moved on and married

the poem and the song
that so many now sing
but you made strong
and gave a lasting ring.

Arlo and Bob Go Fishing

Arlo, whose daddy Woody brought home some big ones, was once talking to Bob. "Hey, Bob," he tells us he said, "why don't you throw some little ones back in?" Arlo makes it sound like there was a pause, a big heavy one, between what he asked and what he hoped Bob might say. We all knew what Arlo was thinking. Here's a guy like Bob, a little slip of a thing, standing on the bank of the river throwing his line in and nonchalantly pulling in these big ones, one after another. Doesn't seem fair. We can see Arlo and other songwriters standing downstream from Bob, waiting for a nibble, praying to hook even a little silver minnow of a song while Bob's pole keeps bending over double. "Yeah, Bob," we're all thinking, "why don't you be nice and throw some of the little ones back in so we can catch something, anything!"

But Bob doesn't bite. I mean he doesn't go for the bait. Bob is one serious, determined, no-nonsense fisherman. Fishing for song is a matter of life and death. No jokes allowed. We all get this, looking up at Arlo from our seats. We're all little guys, throwing our lines into the waters that can be swift or slow, shallow or deep, clear or murky, sunlit or shadow-laden. We're all little guys willing to settle for any catch. We ain't greedy. We want to leave something for the future. We all got mouths to feed, but we know that the other guy's got to eat, too. We'll settle for anything that rises to the bait. And we think it's hilarious that Bob doesn't see how funny this is. Big-fish Bob won't even grin. "Come on, man," Arlo says in that twangy hip argot of speaking he must have inherited from his old man, "cancha throw a few little ones back in so's the rest of us can catch somethin'?" Yeah, Bob, ain't you already caught enough big ones for one lifetime? Isn't there a season limit and a fine for going over it? How's come you gotta be greedy? How could such a little man pull in so many huge songs? What's your trick? What's your secret? Who taught you how to bait the hook and where to drop it into the water?

Makes you wonder if maybe old Woody didn't take Arlo fishing at least a few times and tell his little boy some big ones about the fish that did NOT get away. Like the time he dangled his cane pole in the water and pulled up that monster from the deep, the one whose chorus begins, "This land is your land." Imagine that, pulling in a whole land, a whole country and its people, a whole continent into a single song. Your daddy tells you a tale like that and for the rest of your life you can't help but wonder when the big one's gonna strike. Poor little Arlo. Maybe that's why Bob didn't laugh. Bob held his tongue. He understood.

Song for Bob Dylan

1971

The restless little
Midwestern creature
with reflecting eyes
tingling antennae
and scraping cry
secretes himself in
a new myth for each
winter and then drops
out and wings away
to another tree just
as his followers
begin to wriggle
in the cocoon
that's fallen behind.

Girl of the Hill Country

after Bob Dylan and traditional song

If you're traveling in the hill country
where woods roll as far as you can see
and the sun sets on the hazy Ohio,
say hello to a girl I once loved.

Tell her I remember that wisp of hair
that trailed across big blue eyes,
the way she would say my name
with a voice that rose like a spring.

If you see snowflakes pile on cedar green,
tell me if she still wears that same smile
that makes winter skin tingle when
blood flows oh so slow in your veins.

If you see the old red barns lean
in heat where purple hollyhocks stand,
please ask if she remembers my name,
tell her I dream of coming back home.

If you're traveling in the hill country
when yellow leaves fall, remember me
to one who lives there. My lips still
hold the sound of her name like a hymn.

My Bob Dylan Dreams

He didn't let me be
in his dreams, but he kept
coming back into mine.

Often it was in a house
or backyard where I
protected his privacy.
Never called him Dylan.
Only called him Bob.
He called me Norb.

Bobcats forever sniffin'
on his trail, long lost
brothers creepin' out
of the shadows to
claim their kinship.
Muttering mouths feeding
him his own lines as if
they wrote them themselves.
The press armed with odd-ass
questions nobody could answer.

Ladies of the day and night
giving him that hungry look.
Oracles of the abyss.
Hipsters on high
hankering for Apocalypse
waiting for any sign
or signal to take
whatever kind of action.

We shot hoops together.
He put a nice spin
on his shots, could bank
them in from any angle.
Had some weird moves.
You never knew where

they came from or where
he might go next. You'd
have to say he was good.

He liked it completely quiet.
Liked to fish in streams,
ponds, or lakes, lost for
long times in reveries.
Liked to watch a river
flow or ripples spread
beyond on the surface.

Believe it or not,
he asked me about
poetry, had read some
of what I have written.
So I asked him
about the country blues,
where some of my
poems came from.

Man, you shoulda seen
the light in his eyes!
There was no bottom
to those deep waters
when that little man
talked about the blues.

I won't say we two
were blues brothers,
but we swam together
easily in those waters.

Maybe that's why he
kept coming back
into my dreams,
because he knew
where he could
go for a long swim
and never be hassled.

The Franconian Tambourine Men

for Helmut and Hans

Helmut the poet and Hans the folk singer stand on a tiny stage in a Franconian Rathskeller on an October Sunday night. The audience sits at tables under a vaulted ceiling, sipping beer. As the lights dim, then brighten, Hans the carpenter strums his guitar and launches into Bob Dylan's "Mr. Tambourine Man," as translated by Helmut, in the dialect spoken by my Franconian ancestors. My boot heels are ready for wandering.

I close my eyes and wind down the smoky rings of my mind. I return to the beaches of Long Island where I walked with my children, to the woods of southern Indiana where I hunted with my father, to the chaotic streets of the 1960s where I marched as a student, to the fields of Lower Franconia where my father's forefathers worked as day laborers before they left for the land of blue skies, to the waters of the Main River where my mother's people worked on small boats before they crossed the big water on a larger boat.

Hearing Bob Dylan's rough Minnesota voice under Hans' rustic one, I let myself go down the ruins of time into all these places and times. I listen again to my mother and father speak to one another in a mid-nineteenth-century dialect at the table where we children sat in mid-twentieth-century Indiana. I open my eyes and am led by Bob's tambourine man–pied piper into the Faustian Halloween night where Helmut's Franconian dialect punches the American troubadour's vision along in Hans' strong voice.

Even though I had no destination in mind, these Franconian tambourine men have freed me to go anywhere. I am a man who carries many voices and visions, can dance with one hand waving free, and speak in more languages than one. I am a listener who follows the Minnesota minstrel and his songs that cast a spell on us, set us sailing across the waters, and transport us into worlds within worlds.

Hoosier Dylan

Around here in pioneer days, they say,
if someone knocked on your cabin door,
you asked, "Whose y'er?" That's how
we supposedly came to be called Hoosiers.

Well, folks, here comes Hoosier Dylan.
I ask you, Who's y'er Dylan?
We got plenty to serve up to ya!

We got young folkie Bob comin'
to Greenwich Village in New York City
fresh out of Minnesota sniffin' the trail
of Woody Guthrie of Oklahoma.
We got young whippersnapper bluesman
Bob soundin' as old as the coots in the hills
telling us how he wants to be buried.
We got protestin' Bob slammin' injustice
with images that come from ancient visions.
We got the subterranean urban hipster,
the bohemian Bob who turned on
the electricity, made his hair stand on end,
and let the surreal lines flow like traffic
on Highway 61 until some of his fans called
him Traitor and cried out he was Judas!

We also got for ya recluse Bob,
holed up in the mountains with the sad-
eyed lady of the lowlands as his wife.
We got country Bob crooning to his lady
laying across his big brass bed. Kids one,
two, three, four followed him around as he
sat there watchin' the river flow and played
old time music in the basement with the boys
in the Band, consorted with Mrs. Henry
and Tiny Montgomery, and headed
on over to that million dollar bash,
all the while yearnin' to be released.

And when the marriage started to rip
apart and Bob had to have one more cup
of coffee before descendin' to the valley
below with the Rolling Thunder Revue,
like the Hoosier troupe puttin' on this show,
we brought that Bob along tonight too.
In fact, we also got Gospel Bob,
born yet again to tell ya ya better
serve somebody beside yourself
before the world explodes into hellfire.

We also got the wizened bluesman Bob
hitting the roadhouse night after night
on the endless highway ridin' the tour
bus to a town somewhere near you raspin'
and croakin' like he really *is* ancient.

So who's y'er Dylan? my friends.
If you don't see the Dylan who's y'ers
tonight in this old Hoosier theatre,
let us know and next time we'll be
sure to bring him along and maybe
even the newest Bob lately reinvented,
still busy bein' born after all these years.

HOOSIER DYLAN
THE SONGS OF BOB DYLAN
featuring
GORDON BONHAM
bobbie lancaster
TIM GRIMM
white lightning boys
JENNIE DEVOE
joyous garde
JASON WILBER
norbert krapf
indiana poet laureate
SATURDAY, JANUARY 9
ATHENAEUM THEATER
401 E. Michigan, Indianapolis
$15 in Advance / $18 @ the Door
Doors @ 6:30 / Show @ 7:30
Call 812-603-3503 for Info
Tix at Indy CD & Vinyl and Luna Music

Song of the Blue-Eyed Son

Everybody's blue-eyed son
came out of the small town
but he had the old eye
of a man who could see

wild wolves circling the new-born
baby and he stepped into the mouth
of dozens of graveyards and heard
the clapping thunder and the sound

of people starving and the song
of the poet who died in the gutter
and he knew the executioner's face
will always be well hidden

and he knew his song well before
he started singing and knew
the hard rain was going to fall
and fall and keep on falling

and pellets of poison would
infiltrate the waters and souls
would be forgotten and he stood
alone on the mountain and had

already been where few go
and seen what not many
want to envision and made
songs that fall like acid rain.

The Voice

Some listeners cannot get beyond the voice, which they find awful, even repulsive. Not pretty, not pleasant, not pleasing, even though it is full of feeling. Sometimes sad, sometimes angry and vicious, sometimes exuberant, mischievous, wickedly charming, seductive, on occasion regretful, contrite, full of spiritual longing. This is a cracked, smoke-ravaged voice that tells a tale that could take place in any time or place. This is a voice that talks at least as much as it sings, shoe-spooning red-hot word after word into its narrative lines, turns on itself, takes detours and diversions, spins on the rocks and almost veers into the ditch, but finds its way back to the main road whenever it must. This voice has the talking blues and has got it right!

This voice is a ragged, nasal, phlegm-ball of a voice that can clear its throat, spit out its imperfections, and croon when it wants to. This voice won't win the Pulitzer or Nobel Prize, but the song it sings uses it to serve its ends and bring the vision home. This voice is blue, often a dark and bruised blue, feels around the floor for its shoes at the crack of dawn, smells the coffee brewing downstairs, lights up a cigarette, coughs a few times, and begins an old talking blues song that turns into something new. This voice chants demonic and angelic subterranean poetry from the back pew.

If you worship pretty, this voice simply won't do. If you must have sugary and sweet to flavor your coffee or tea, forget this voice. But if you like a rough whiskey voice that knows how to crank up the mystery, take you into the dark, pull you down to the bottom, then lift you into the light that you have trouble finding on your own, this voice may have something to say to you.

This voice may teach you a new way to hear a song that was previously beyond your frequency range. This voice may enable you to see a vision you never had. Beware of giving into this voice – which you thought does not know how to sing. Be careful: This voice is dangerous! This voice is wily, wild, and wise. This voice knows what it is doing, even though you may be convinced it does not. Be forewarned: This voice could take you where you thought you never wanted to go. If you can get beyond an addiction to the merely pretty, this voice could change your life.

This Time 'Round

for Kriss & Greg

When love comes calling
you may be in the middle
of a song you have sung
but never really heard.

You begin with "I Want You"
but the set list slips
out the window and it's
"I'll Be Your Baby Tonight."

That big fat moon is shinin'
like a you know what.
Yeah, go on and bring that
bottle right on over here.

Now it's "Lay Lady Lay"
in a beautiful big brass bed.
All the colors of the rainbow
shine in both your heads.

You tell her she's an artist
who won't ever look back.
You'll be proud to steal her
anything she'll ever need.

She's no longer "Tangled Up in Blue."
You are her "Mr. Tambourine Man,"
she wants to follow you, has lost
her "Subterranean Homesick Blues."

This time you both know you
are not gonna throw it all away.
You can make time to work and play.
This time 'round love is gonna stay.

You are bringing it all back home,
pledging your time to one another.
Love came calling again and this time
'round you'll keep it "Forever Young."

The Gift

Once an interviewer
asked Bob Dylan if he
ever talked to anyone
about his belief as a youth
that he had a gift that
would find its light
beyond his small town

and he looked up
and opened his eyes
more fully and said,
No, no, you don't
want to do that

because if you do
you make yourself
vulnerable and what
you feel is delicate
and could be killed
before it comes out.

And you keep it
to yourself, he might
have added, until others
can see what you have
to give, but he didn't,

and you could see
by the light in his eyes
at that moment

why he lets his songs
speak for themselves
and reveal in their
unique way his gift.

Tambourine Man in Hell's Kitchen

You step into the lights
on the stage in the industrial
building and bark out hard
that you are again changing
your way of thinking and doing.
You love it, don't you, that you
are back in Hell's Kitchen where
you can howl the blues and croon
the country under a full moon.
No name outside on the building,
no name high on the marqee.
Your name it ain't nothing,
your age now means even less.
The small house that is full
is all on its feet, no seats allowed
in this prison cell of a black hole.
You stand there staring back
in your River Boat Gambler
cum Preacher man in white
cowboy hat and boots uniform
topped off with a sharp bola tie.
You can be, bearing down on seventy,
Tangled Up in Blue out on Desolation
Row where T. S. Eliot and Ezra Pound
spar and spit in the Captain's Tower
above an Infiniti showroom and your
old pal Shakespeare raps in the alley
in iambic pentameter where circus
performers toss their Thunderbird
wine bottles that clank on concrete
or crash into shards that shine
in the light of the Mexican moon.
You been to Juarez where hungry
women made a mess out of you
and it's time, it's way past time
to come back to New York City,

even though revolution is no longer
in the acid air. If your heart has gone
forgetful, it still beats big and loud
out on Highway 61 along the Hudson.
You say you Ain't Talkin', but how
much louder could one man talk
on surging keyboards, staccato
guitar, percussive and obsessive
moutharp, and a voice that rasps
and chants, barks and bellows out
onto the street where the song
is the sun and the moon exerts
its pull and you are the diminutive
poet with the powerful vision hell-
bent on prophesy still with a beat
that smashes up against concrete
and echoes in moonlit alleys.

Letter to Bob Dylan with One Eye Closed

In Manny's Music Store,
156 West 48th Street,
Manhattan, New York

you signed the picture
of yourself as rock hipster
with your right fist

closed over your right
eye and wrote: *To Manny,*
Keep one eye closed

at all cost. As I walk
into my study before
dawn to write a poem

that came to me
in the dark, I keep
one eye closed,

one eye open,
nod at your impish
picture to the right

of the door,
and go down into
the world behind

your fist and closed
eye to bring back up
from the deep dark

whatever light
and silence you
left for me to find.

BOB DYLAN

The Day John Lennon

The day John Lennon . . .
we were living in Germany,
had recently adopted a baby girl
from Colombia, and were happy
even though I was laid up in bed
with a painful sinus infection.

The day John Lennon . . .
we did not listen to the news
on the radio or turn on the TV
or talk to any friends on the phone
or neighbors in the apartment building
because I was sick in bed and we
just tried to take care of ourselves
and nurse our little world back
to routine health so we could
get ready for Christmas in Germany.

The day John Lennon . . .
it was the 8th of December,
the feast of the Immaculate Conception,
a holy day of obligation for Catholics,
but we did not leave our apartment
and I made it no farther from the bed
than to tiptoe to the bathroom
or to the kitchen table to sip
a bowl of chicken noodle soup.

The day before John Lennon . . .
our dear friend in New York
who was planning to visit us
when the German winter was over
went out and bought a Christmas tree
that she propped in the corner
of her studio apartment.

One day later she wrote a letter
in which she told us she would
not be able to put one single
ornament on her Tannenbaum.

The day after John Lennon . . .
I went in to work, stopped
to buy a newspaper, and read
the headline boldly proclaiming
that John Lennon had been . . .
When I reached my office,
I picked up the phone, dialed
our apartment number, and told
my wife something terrible
had happened: John Lennon had been . . .
"That's not supposed to happen,"
she said after a painfully long silence.
"No it isn't!" was all I could add.

All day after the day John Lennon . . .
all I could hear was the tune
and the lyrics of a song I loved
in which John Lennon tried to imagine
the kind of world I wanted to give
to my daughter, and now that she is
26 years old, I still hope and pray
that our children and hers will dream
and that we can learn to live as one.

Pig Belly Blues

for Yank Rachell

Sooiee, sooiee, got me a mandolin for my little pig.
Sooiee, sooeie, bought a mandolin with my little pig.
Mama's sure angry but her little boy's thinkin' big.

You ever pluck the blues on a little pig's belly?
You ever play the blues on a little pig's belly?
Mandolin blues can turn a mama to grape jelly.

Well, I pluck my mandolin from the bottom up.
Yeah, I pluck and strum her from the bottom up.
She sounds good when I stroke her from the bottom up.

Yeah, you can go and call me Yank.
Yessir, go right ahead and call me Yank.
Yank's mandolin got beaucoup blues in the tank.

Came up to Indy all the way from West Tennessee,
Came up to Indy all the way from West Tennessee.
Mandolin and the pig belly blues came along with me.

Once you feel the blues it won't ever stop.
Once you sing the blues it don't ever stop.
Got blues in your head till the day you drop.

Still hear Hammie and Sleepy John with me on the stage.
Still hear Big Joe and Sonny Boy with me on the stage.
The old-time down-home blues always for me the rage.

Still got the taste of moonshine whiskey on my tongue
Still taste some a that moonshine whiskey on my tongue.
White whiskey been on my mind since I was young.

My woman fed me biscuits baked before break of day.
My woman gave me biscuits baked before break of day.
Taste those biscuits and white moonshine when I play.

Yank's a deep-diving duck for the moonshine blues.
Yank's mouth be always open for hot biscuit blues.
Yank's mandolin is forever full of the pig belly blues.

Sweet Home Indianapolis

for Brenda Williams

Well, I'm going back home to Indianapolis.
This girl's coming back home to Indianapolis
though it ain't the world's biggest metropolis.

Now I don't want any of your shameless pity
says Indy ain't no New York or Kansas City.
For favorite city my hometown heart says Indy.

Yeah, I heard plenty of city blues in Chicago.
I heard and sang plenty of blues up in Chicago
but back home to Indy is where I want to go.

You want to know about my favorite spot?
You want to know what's my favorite spot?
Hah, it's where the music cooks red-hot!

On a street corner stands a man in a white suit.
On a street corner stands a man in a white suit.
My baby's nothin' but a bowl of fresh fruit.

I'm gonna join my man and head out for the Avenue.
Soon as it's dark we're gonna walk down the Avenue
in style ready to hear Wes play the Naptown Blues.

We're gonna hear Freddy Hubbard and J. J. Johnson.
We're gonna hear Freddy Hubbard and J. J. Johnson.
Ain't no kinda jazz we ain't got goin' down in this town!

I'm already on my way back home to Indianapolis.
I'm at least halfway back home to Indianapolis,
proud to say Indy's my number one metropolis.

Jennie's Song

When you sing for us
your hair burns bright
like a bonfire in the dark.

Your voice takes flight
and lifts us with you
beyond a dreary day.

What you do, you do
with such heart and soul
it flows like a transfusion

of blood to make us whole.
You lay on us a sultry mix
of the sensual and the spiritual

that gives us more than kicks
and makes us feel so good
we come crying for more.

In our downtown neighborhood,
drawing on a deep old well
you transport us far away.

Your voice, like a groundswell,
moves us to an opening beyond
where we sway as if entranced.

Your feet remain on the ground
however high your visions go.
You make us feel forever young.

We chant your name, Jennie DeVoe.
Your gifts and staying power abound.
Glory be your soulful song is sung.

Jack's Song

Little boy born
with big eyes
and a wide smile
near the banks
of the ancient river
that flows through
your hometown,

you came into
the world bobbing
on the currents
of song your mama
and daddy sing
in such sweet harmony

the country angels stop
flying and land
on the ground and sit
and listen to the lyrics
your parents wrote
one after the other
from the heart
they gave to you.

When you learn
how to walk
the banks of
the old Oh-hi-oh,
you will have
visions of flatboats
that once floated
by your hometown
on their way toward
the hills where I was
born and grew up.

Named after your
grand-daddy Jack
who played the bass,
you will see a family
with six children
come all the way
from Germany to
find a new home
in the hills I love.

Sing them a song,
boy with the smile
as wide as the river,

make them feel
at home in this
always new world
where love flows
slow and steady
and meanders around
the bends that
come our way

with an invisible
power that moves
us on and makes us
turn our ears to
the harmonies of your
mama and daddy's song
that lives in your voice
and stays in our ears.

Someone Who Misses New Orleans

Do you know what it means to miss New Orleans?
as sung by Louis Armstrong

I know someone
who knows what it means
to miss New Orleans,
the visits to relatives
who lived in a small shotgun house
on Freret Street, in Uptown,
played canasta there with cousins, slurped
snow cones from a neighborhood stand.

I know someone
who knows what it means
to miss New Orleans,
who as a college student
drove down Robert E. Lee Boulevard,
not far from Lake Ponchatrain,
to a college that no longer exists,
looking at pink oleander in bloom,
someone who loves crepe myrtle
and camellia and magnolia
and still believes summer begins in March,
though March is a cruel month up North.

I know someone
who knows what it means
to miss New Orleans,
who married a young man from Indiana,
which happens to rhyme with Louisiana,
who waited for him to fly down to meet
her Cajun family for the first time,
eat crawfish stew, Mississippi River shrimp,
gumbo, okra, and stuffed eggplant,
sip strong coffee from a family demitasse
and just made it back out of the airport

on the very last flight before
Hurricane Camille hit with her full fury.

I know someone
who knows what it means
to miss New Orleans,
who felt a diamond ring being slipped
on her finger on a bench in City Park,
under the live oaks and Spanish moss,
who brought her new husband to stay
in her brother's apartment
in the Pontalbo Building, on Jackson Square,
near St. Louis Cathedral and sip café au lait
and savor beignet in the Café du Monde like
a new communicant, as jazz oozed and pulsed
out of every building in the all-night French Quarter.

I know what it means
to know someone
who misses New Orleans,
someone who married a young man
who brought her to live far away
from home, in New York, leaving
her mother sad but too proud to complain.

I know someone
who knows what it means
to miss New Orleans,
because when her mother and father
married they moved to the city
from the country and lived
on Tonti Street in Mid-City and ate
red beans and rice every Monday for dinner;
and one day many years later,
in another part of the United States,
as Katrina whirled across the Gulf,
she turned on the TV, watched the waters
of the Lake and the Gulf batter the levee,
and silently sobbed as the waters rose

up the sides of houses and buildings,
winds howling through the live oaks.

I know someone
who knows what it means
to return to New Orleans
with beloved old friends
to drive up and down streets
in Lakeview, Bucktown,
the Lower Ninth Ward, and Arabi
and see houses blown off
their concrete blocks, trees twisted
and crashed onto roofs, windows
blasted out by winds, everyday
objects of ordinary lives scattered,
piled and heaped everywhere like
rubble in a war-ravaged country.

I know someone
who knows what it means
to miss New Orleans and come back
and see painted on the wall
of a condemned house, on the front porch,
a red, white, and blue American flag,
with a hand-painted caption below,
GOD BLESS AMERICA.

I also know what it means
to come back with someone
who loves New Orleans
and finds jazz the heartbeat
of a Sunday mass celebrated
by an African American priest
with a Cajun name, in Tremé,
in St. Augustine Church,
in a parish the Catholic authorities
had decreed would be eliminated,
before the people refused to let it die
because the spirit of God

shook their bodies to the core as,
to the backing of trumpet, saxophone,
guitar, banjo, bass, piano, and drum,
they sang hymns and spirituals
that lifted their spirits and made them
believe deep in their hearts that
we are all children of God
who want to be among that number
and whose spirits shall rise higher
than the waters and winds of any storm
named after any man or woman,
or generations of injustice,
could ever bring down to
the ground and keep down low.

The Night the Guitarist Broke Loose

for Peter and Monika

Maybe the moon was right
as well as all the lights blinking
in the dark Indiana sky

but everything was also in place
inside the lounge where a film
crew was ready as he stood

in position on stage where the drummer's
hands held the sticks high ready to pound
a beat and the violinist's bow was ready

to smoke across hot strings and the key-
boardist's fingers were poised to strike,
to ignite black and white. It was

her band and he was her man and she
said "Rock out, man!" His guitar
newly let loose made sounds nobody

had ever heard it make: it honked,
it wailed, it caterwauled, it careened,
fuzzed up and fooled around

the corners of the notes and blended
and blurred and bent everything
and sent sound in another direction.

His leg slung out and came back
to the stage floor, the audience
let itself howl its approval in the kind

of animal sounds that were escaping
from his guitar, the film crew
smiled and the keyboardist sat

facing her husband and her jaw
dropped, her smile spread
as she pounded him on, and his

guitar kept climbing and reaching
and sassing and almost sobbing
before resolving itself into a mad

hieroglyphic of sound on the night
that the woman keyboardist-leader
of the band let her husband rock out.

All the animals in the cold crawled
out of their lairs and sat up and listened
as if Orpheus had descended into their

midst and the audience inside found
their hands pounding together in ways
they never had and love was in the air

and the guitar spoke a language it must
have known but was never before
set loose and there was a hooting

tongue in the mouth of every
man and woman who listened.
The guitarist grinned and bowed

and after the last encore when friends
came up to compliment him he said:
"I just do whatever she lets me do."

4 *Moon of Falling Leaves*

Bavarian Blue

I'm on the train by myself in Bavaria,
don't know how I got there or where
I'm going, except back into my past.

My journal open on my lap, I record
what I see and feel, to share with
anyone who may one day care

to read or listen. I look out
at the landscape and see something
I can almost not believe, stands

of unending wild lupine, spikes
of dry purplish blue around every
bend, climbing every bank as if

rising up to touch me where I sit,
this flower that people in the country
where I was born would die to grow

in their garden. Here it is everywhere,
like wild weeds gone out of control,
free to the eye to take in, to ingest,

this cornucopia of dark color left
behind by the ancestors who departed,
perhaps brought along in memory

and talked about until the dark blue
faded into oblivion. Here out
in the countryside between villages

this deep haunting color takes me
in its grip and pulls me back off this
train into the Bavarian fields

that once had names to those who
worked them for others, like my
day-laborer ancestors, who must

have worshiped these wild mysterious
flowers, so hearty they take root
anywhere, must have missed them

when they entered the shade-flooded,
tree-thick southern Indiana wilderness,
must have missed and longed for what

I now see everywhere, over and over,
as the rails curve and climb and swerve
through this countryside I love as if

I once curled a scythe in these fields
and pulled a rake. When I fall
asleep tonight I will be back in bed

in a cottage where animals breathe
between the same walls where I see
wild lupine bloom beneath my eyelids.

Eberhard Reichmann at Peter's Gate

He's following in the footsteps
of all the German immigrants
whose stories he helped to tell.

As he passes, they greet him,
give him a Wurst and stein of beer,
say once more, *Auf Wiedersehen.*

At Heaven's Door, he teaches
St. Peter how to sing the immortal
hymns in Swabian dialect.

The Great Gate swings open,
the heavenly choir sings,
and Eb's voice leads the way

as we follow in his footsteps
singing with him the lyrics
he led us back to with gusto.

Fire in a Horse Trough

Lohr am Main

Cobblestones on the street where
my maternal ancestors once lived.

Before an ancient cottage, a horse
watering trough filled with black earth.

Carved in sandstone, the year 1836 – four
years before they left. *Going to America,*

going to America! Above in pink profusion
a row of geraniums with dark green leaves.

Taller geraniums behind burning red. Back,
I am back from America, have come back

all the way over an ocean to be in their town
of Lohr am Main and walk down their narrow

street to the river below, on which they worked
on boats for many generations. Eyes full of

shadows rising to the surface, I drink hard
of Franconian flames in the horse trough.

Questions on a Wall

on the occasion of the twentieth anniversary
of the fall of the Berlin Wall

If there is something that does not love
a wall, is there also not something that
hates a wall and wants it down as soon
as someone else puts it up to keep some
people in and some people out of wherever
they may live or want to live? Why and who
and what is it wants to keep people apart,
friend from friend, relative from relative,
lover from lover, husband from wife,
parent from child, stranger from stranger,
no matter what tongue they speak,
even if it is the same language?

Is there not something about a wall that
encourages people to come out singly
or in pairs or even in packs in the dark
to prowl and write or spray-paint in primary
colors cartoon figures and sayings and slashings,
questions and imperatives of one kind or another
on this stark and hideous man-made concrete barrier:
WARUM HABT IHR DAS GEMACHT?
WHY HAVE YOU MADE/DONE THIS?
Who are you, who, who, who are you,
who are you and why? *WARUM HABT IHR*
DAS GEMACHT? WHY HAVE YOU
MADE/DONE THIS? Who are you?
Who am I? Why are you you and not I?
Am I not you? Are you not I?

If good fences or walls make good neighbors,
how do we know a good from a bad fence?
What language would we use to tell one another
the difference between good and bad?

Why a no-man's-land between
you and me, us and them, her and him?
Between me, myself and I? A no-man's-
land where white crosses stood at night
in the artificial light and in broad daylight
bearing the names, Heinz Sokolowski,
or lack of names, *Unbekannt*/Unknown;
Marienetta Jirkowski, *Unbekannt.*
And who shot Heinz, who shot Marienetta,
who shot *Unbekannt* and how many times
before his or her heart stopped beating?
Whose finger pulled the trigger? Did you?
Did I? Did they do it? What did the two
squinting eyes see as the finger squeezed?

Does Marienetta lie at the foot of her cross?
Heinz at the foot of his? Do the Unknowns
rest at the foot of theirs? Who comes to pray
for her, him, them? Did their mothers and fathers
know what happened to their children?
Who remembers the dead as *Kinder*?
When you read or hear this read,
can you see fingers clutching over the top
of the wall and Heinz's or Marienetta's face
appear in the full bloom of hope as they
crawl over the wall thinking they have finally
made it home to freedom, wherever it
may live, only to be cut down and dumped
dead into a black hole in no-man's-land?

Who or what is a No Man? A No Woman?
Are we all a No Man or Woman somewhere?
How many *Unbekannte* shot down
in no-man's-land does it take
before any *Unbekannt* becomes known
to be at least a someone or comes to know
he's no longer a man? How many walls
must we put up and take down before
we can all be free? How can we put

Marienetta, Heinz, and the Unknowns
back together? How long will it take
to understand why there is something
that does not love a wall, that wants
it down, down, down, and we all shout
with the students and the children,

Die Mauer muss weg.
Die Mauer muss weg.
The wall must come down.
Down with the wall!

Patoka Visions

In the waters
of the Patoka
I have seen

human blood
and poison bubbles.
In the winter woods

I have seen
hanging on bare
branches the flesh

of our sons and
daughters burned
beside the waters

of the Tigris
and Euphrates.
Babylon is

everywhere on
my mind and in
the hills I hear

the wailing
of women
and children

turned out of
their homes by
those who pray,

in a slightly
different way,
to the same gods.

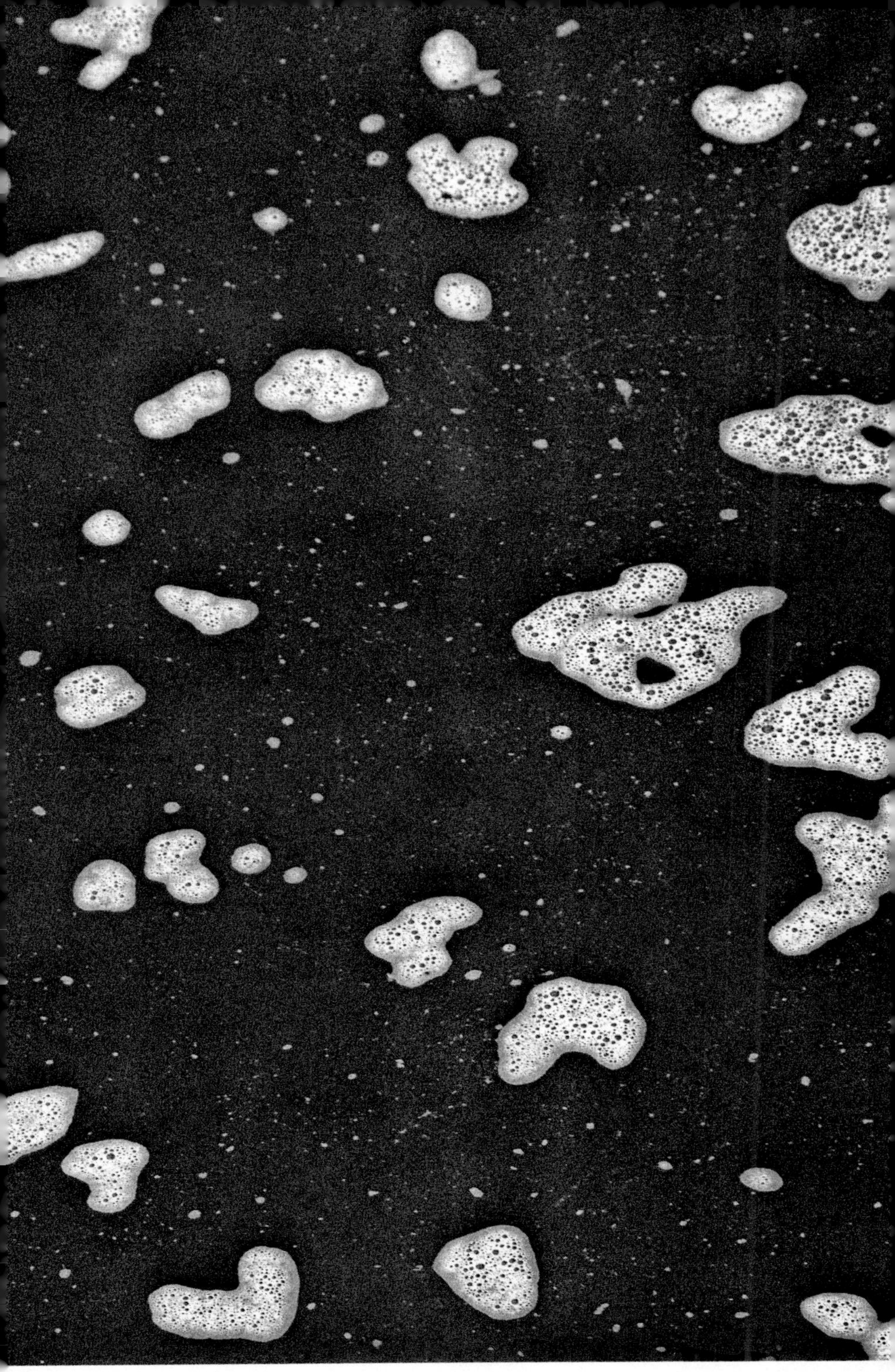

The Diner Was Gone

I went to the diner,
but the diner was gone.
So were the people
I always saw there.

I walked to the church,
but it had not moved.
Massive sandstone blocks
and tulip poplar columns
stay put a long time.

I carried on to the cemetery
and everybody who was present
the last time was still there,
but a bunch of new people
had since then moved in.

I said hello to everybody I knew,
offered a prayer on their behalf,
asked them not to move away
before I joined the community.

I think I heard them promise
they would always stay put.
Somehow I find the dead
easier to believe than the living.

For a long-term investment,
I put my money on the dead.
They are in it for the long haul,
don't pull out when it grows dark.

Blind Man, Blind Man

Blind man, blind man,
tell me a story
of a man trying
to get home after
a long war.

Tell me how he
outwitted a one-eyed
monster who devoured
his men like candy.

Tell us what you see,
blind man, that the rest
of us cannot.

Tell us about
the Scylla and Charybdis
that we must somehow
learn to sail between,
the rocks in the high
and deep raging seas.

Blind man, blind man,
tell me about the woman
who waits for me
in the house I built
while suitors woo her,
drink my wine,
and plow my field
as the wildcat howls
in the winds at night
and riders approach.

Tell me, tell me
about the beautiful
Circe who lures me
with her womanly
powers and keeps me

and my men on her island
until she releases me
to go find my mother
who has departed to
the realm of spirits
in the waters of the north
while I have been gone.

Blind man, blind man,
how you see inside me?
How you know so well
what hurts me so bad,
what drives me home
to the land I love?

Blind man, blind man,
sing me home,
sailor, soldier, lover,
father, mere mortal
whose eyes cannot
see so far inside myself
as your dead blind orbs
so easily cut through.

Tell me your story,
Homer, give me your
power to speak
for the people,
to tell the story
all would hear.

Tell my lover
I come home
to touch her again,
look into her eyes
so soft and green.

Tell my people
I love them as much
as I love the land

where I was born
that calls me back.

Blind man, blind man,
give me voice,
give me vision,
give me the courage
to find my way
back home to all
that I inherited
when I came forth
from the womb.

Give me your eyes,
blind man,
lend me your voice
so I can sing
to the gods
and the goddesses
who look down
on me and my people
from above

and petition them
for mercy to let us
come and be together
once again, one family,
one nation, a people
devoted to the place
where we live.

Sit with me, blind man,
Herr Homer, as the fire
burns in the night.
Touch me like
the father you are.
Whisper in my ear.

Help me hear again
the morning song

of my patient wife,
the violin of my daughter,
the lyre of my son,
the song of the birds
in the tree that arches
over the bedroom
in which my love
and I wake in one
another's arms.

Blind man, blind man,
Homer of my heart,
I am weary and my
time is growing short.
Sing me back home
to the land I love.

The County Historian and the Town Drunk

in memory of John Fierst

He knew the history
of all families that settled
in his place. He knew
which families married
into one another, who
everyone's father and mother
was, and could tell stories
about each and every one.

In the high school,
he taught the bigger history,
the history of the county,
the state, the nation
of nations, but always
he kept his finger
on the pulse of the place
he never wanted to leave.

In his basement he kept
all the books and papers
everyone passed on to him.
He knew where every book,
magazine, and newspaper
article could be found.
Ask him a question about
any family, any farm,
any event over the years
and he disappeared into
the archives in the basement
and came back up the stairs
with the answer, free of charge.

Ask him the name of the family
that owned the farm on the ridge
above the lake where the Boy Scout

camp once was, since they came
over from Germany, and their woods
where your father took you to hunt
squirrels the first time when
you were a boy, and he dug up
the name in the plat records
shelved in order in the archives.

Ask him who played second
in what year on the town's
semi-pro baseball team
or guard on the state championship
basketball team and he gave you
the first and last name and mother's
and father's names and on what
street they lived and when the kid
graduated from high school, whom
he married, how many kids they have,
the color of the house they live in,
and what kind of work he does today.

His humor was as dry as the bones
of a possum killed on a back road
on top of a hill and left to bleach
in the hot August sun. Every time
you passed, you saw more white.
If you knew what to look for,
you could find a sly grin hiding
somewhere on that straight face.

Once the niece of my favorite
high school English teacher,
Jack Leas, wrote to order
copies of my book published
by the county historical society
and said to say hello to her uncle.
For decades, John was the heart
and soul of the society, though
he kept his name and title quiet.

When the county museum started up,
you could not keep him out of it.
His wife joked that they ought
to give him a bed to sleep in.

When I met the English teacher's
niece to read my poems at her
university, she told me that along
with copies of my books arrived
a note in the county historian's
hand explaining that "the only
Jack Leas I know is the town drunk."

Jack the Ripper

There was this great teacher named
Jack London Leas. After we graduated

from high school and began to pal
around with him, we called him

Jack the Ripper. Went to his house,
some of us, to listen to classical music,

discuss literature, and once in a while
argue politics, sex, and religion,

not always in that order. Drank
a lot of beer, sometimes hard stuff.

He loved the romantics like Tchaikovsky,
but also Bach and Beethoven. He played

the piano and also organ but hated
what he called pop music, rock.

What a sharp tongue he had.
His irony could go on and on.

Some folks were afraid of him
just because he was big and tall,

bald head, bushy eyebrows, and a big
paunch that he carried like a loaded

wheelbarrow. Took great big steps
that ate up the sidewalk, as if he were

about to climb up the walls of the PO
like King Kong. Couldn't see worth

a damn, wore thick glasses, squinted
so some thought he was always angry

but he was just kinda blind. Lived all
by his lonesome. Liked company.

Could bark like a dog if he thought
you disagreed with him and didn't

know any better. "God damn it,
I said she was hideously ugly!"

he once insisted about a woman
who did not appeal to him.

He was a great teacher for some
but he intimidated those who

were not secure in who and what
they were. His old college friend,

a fellow teacher he called Woody,
would come to visit in the summer

and they would reminisce about
the time they had to write up their

philosophy of education for a prof.
"At the heart of every student," Woody

would begin, and Ripper continued,
"buried deep in his innermost self,

lies a kernel of nothing but S-H-I-T."
And they would cackle and howl.

Once on a Monday morning he came
in the side door of his long classroom

lugging his hardcover copy of *War and Peace.*
"All right turn them in," he barked with a bite.

If I can't read the s.o.b. you sure
as hell won't be able to either."

When he and his friend the prosecuting
attorney would meet outside the PO

on their way to collecting their mail,
it was like a shoot-out at high noon

on Main Street. "Hello, Leas," Mr. PA
would say, "I see you're again your usual

ugly, cheerful self!" Old Ripper replied,
"Know what you can do to yourself,

you ignorant, unread, uncultivated s.o.b.?"
And the PA would bow as he passed inside.

Once Ripper and I went to see Jack Lemmon
in "Days of Wine and Roses," a flick about

an alcoholic that was such a downer
we bought a pint of peppermint schnapps

and got ourselves sloshed in his living room
discussing the sad implications of the film.

When I backed out of his driveway
at 1:20 AM, my back tire caught

some branches of the neighbor's shrub.
Mrs. X called to report she had seen

a deranged drunk back over her bush.
Ripper laughed so hard he like to wet

himself, is the way he put it. When he died,
almost forty years after I graduated from

high school, I flew back home
from New York to be his pallbearer.

At the meal after his funeral,
I read a poem about the time

a bunch of us listened to classical
organ music in his living room

while drinking beer and decided to
drive down to the big Romanesque

church in the center of town to hear
him play the big organ in the loft.

Had our own private concert. Jack
had read the poem and loved it.

I could feel him grinning from beyond.
He came to every poetry reading

I ever gave in town and then tagged
along with a bunch of us for beer.

I can still see him walk the sidewalks
and hear him bark and bitch at the PA

who was also one of the pallbearers
and joked his turn would come next.

By God it sure did, a few months later.

Maybe I Knew Him

Maybe I knew him,
maybe I didn't,
the father who came home
from a Louisville hospital
after having shock treatment.

Maybe I did understand,
maybe I did not grasp
why he sat in the white-oak
rocker in our living room
as tears leaked out of his eyes
and no words came from his mouth.

Maybe I did understand
somewhat while I also regretted
why the father I loved
inched the car into the garage
and tried to nudge my basketball
out of the way, without having
to get out of his 1952 blue Dodge,
and left me with a lopsided
basketball that could not be fixed.

Maybe even then I understood
as a kid how and why you
have to adjust your shot
when the ball is off center
and feels awkward to the touch.

Maybe I knew I had to make
an adjustment that came from
somewhere in the dark.
Maybe it just happened,
but I've believed ever since
the day my father nudged
that ball aside there's a way
to make your shot from

any spot or odd angle
even when the ball tilts
to one side and doesn't bounce
the way they say it should.

Maybe I understood that
you do not share this with others
but practice extra hard until
even a lopsided ball feels good
in your hands and you learn how
to spin it the way you want it to
and it drops through the hoop
and touches net on the inside
just as well as all the balls
in the world that are still round.

Missing the Turn

We didn't travel well then
because of the accident
that had left him with
a mangled knee and limp.

He drove, she navigated,
and any city, even
the Louisville she had
lived in, became a menace.

"Turn here!" she would
announce. "Why can't
you give a guy a warning?"
he fumed as he drove past

where he should have turned.
We cowered in the back seat.
Once, decades later, my brother
and I reenacted an early expedition.

Home from New York, I drove
him from southern Indiana
to the Louisville airport, from
which he would return to Florida.

We were mocking our whole
family drama. "Turn here, turn
here!" my brother insisted.
Honest to God, it was too late

to turn into the airport entrance
I soon saw in the rearview mirror.
"Why the hell can't you just give
a guy a warning?" I blurted.

The Screech Owl's Call

There was a screech owl
in a tree over the creek
in the woods behind the house

and at night my brother
and I would lie
on our backs in beds

in rooms separated by a wall
and listen to that tremulous
descending cry from the depths

of the dark. Now that
my brother, more than
half a century later,

has withdrawn from his
brothers and sister, I wonder
what call he hears in the dark.

Beneath the Stones

Is it any accident that walking
in this field makes me feel
connected to those who lived
off what they grew, tended,
and slaughtered, and that going
deeper into these woods reminds
me of the grandfather and great-grand-
father who knew how to kill animals
that lived in these dying trees to feed
their families in a time when a black-
berry was a fruit that grew on a briar
that could prick your fingertip and make
blood ooze if you did not know where
not to put it, or could give you
a sweetness that bursts on your tongue,

just as what you did and when
and where you did it in relation
to the sun and the moon and their
cycles determined how well you
lived on a planet whose resources
were more than adequate to support
anyone who understood and respected
what comes and goes and returns

and honors the stones that do not
give us anything we need unless
we turn them over and take them
away exposing what lives beneath
them even though we do not have
the eyes to perceive the universe
in which what is infinitely smaller
than ourselves comes and goes

millions of times outside the time
we consider our own to name
and manage and manipulate
though our powers be more
limited than we can fathom?

Eating Your Shadow

No matter how fast you run your shadow keeps up.
Rumi

I am running in place
trying to look and feel calm

but my stomach and colon
tell me a different story.

I know I am eating my shadow
and my digestive system is

registering a protest in a way
that my mind cannot control.

Even at midnight I can see
and feel the shadow enter me.

This is a shadow that has broken
off from the rays of the sun.

Any time of day or night
this shadow can pass through.

I know this shadow comes from my son,
who does not perceive his darkness,

or at least what it means. He feels it
is unreal and assigned to him by others.

He prays for me to accept and love
him despite his darkness, and I do,

but love is not the whole story.
The shadow he brings sometimes

eats at him, but he always thinks
it comes from outside and beyond him.

The shadow is all his enemies,
the tormenters who plot against him.

He asks me what to do and I try
to find as many ways as I can

to tell him that the shadow will
abate and relent only if he sees it

for what it is and acknowledges it
and feeds it the credit it craves.

He looks at me and wonders what
I mean, for he can see that a shadow

also has his father in its grip and makes
him double up in pain and he sometimes

suspects and fears he could be the shadow
that holds his father in its silent power.

I try to tell him we all carry a shadow
within ourselves and must learn to feed

it what neutralizes it in order to make
peace with it, but I can tell that my

poor words only partly succeed.
Sometimes it gives me and my son

a temporary respite when I admit
that I'm only partly successful

at living with my own shadow.
That's when our shadows hug

and say they love one another,
but love is never the whole story.

Promethian Prayer: To a Hawk

You are the shadow
that floats in the sky
above where I lie
on my back squinting.

Come down now.
Descend on me while
you can still help.

Come on, cut loose
these entrails with
your butcher beak.

Peck and slash and pull
out all this stench
at the center of me.
Consume this darkness.

Gorge yourself on
what eats at me.

Leave me behind
as bleached bone
whose spirit has been
released to soar
back home to ether.

Dream While My Son Is in the Hospital

I stand outside at night,
in the cold, when I hear
a wounded cry pulsing
in underbrush before me.

An injured bird, a dove,
flutters out of the bush
and hobbles past me
before I can pick it up.

I turn back to the bush,
hear an even more intense
cry of pain from within,
of a small mammal,

when a silvery brown animal
that looks like a mix of wolf,
coyote, fox, and wild dog
with soft brown eyes

steps out before me. It
sits on haunches, looks
at me with sad eyes. "You
should not do that!" I say.

Before I can find the other
mammal crying in the bush,
I am lifted up a chute
to a much higher level

and stumble out onto a snow-
covered landscape. My glasses
fall before I regain my balance.
I reach around for them in the snow,

my fingertips find their stems
as I hear the welcome cry
of an owl above. I hold
the frosted glasses up,

behold in a cone of vision
a great white owl soaring
in a circle high above
in a midnight blue sky

near the top of the world.
His huge wings spread wide,
the owl cries, "He will be
well. He shall be released."

What She Liked

She liked to sing The Tennessee Waltz.
She liked the way Marty Robbins sang.
She liked to watch Dolly Parton's TV show
while my father squirmed in his chair.
She liked to feed cardinals cracked corn
and pick Bibb lettuce from the cold frame.
She remembered growing up on the farm
and the day her daddy died when she was six.
She remembered stirring the corn mash
down in the woods beyond the pasture.
She remembered reading James Whitcomb
Riley's poems in the limbs of a sugar maple.
She talked about how kind her husband had been.
She said they both gave one another leather coats
on the first Christmas Eve they shared together.
She reminisced about their first date on the night
the Calumet Lake Pavilion opened its doors
and they danced together into the wee hours.
She came to every one of my football games
and tried to run onto the field when I made a tackle
with my helmet and staggered to the wrong huddle.
She lit candles and palms when the lightning flashed,
the thunder crashed, and the rain beat against our roof.
She hummed when she washed dishes, made dumplings
on the kitchen table and let them dry in the sunlight.
She let the blackberry cobbler cool on the window sill.
Her daily highlight was always the local news at noon.
She never moved away from where she was born
but did go on trips to visit her children and grandchildren.
She liked to sing Goodnight, Irene and The Tennessee Waltz,
and the music she loved the most came from the country.

What Remains

I never forget
the pawpaws
I gathered

or the blackberries
and persimmons
I picked

or the quail
that exploded
into flight

as I came near
or the baby rabbits
squiggly in their nest

in the back yard
or the ferns
that unfurled

where the woods
began just where
the lawn ended

and I listen
still for the doves
that sang at dusk

at the back
of the garden
behind where

the potatoes
swelled large
underground.

Wild Onion

Always liked to
chew tangy tube
of wild onion.

Mother served
salads of tender
dandelion leaves.

Father fermented
wine of black-
berries I picked.

We ate wild
animals of
forest and field.

Sassafras tea
circulated well
in our blood.

If we are what
we eat and drink,
I am my place.

Come with Me

Come with me, come with me,
let's walk into the wild woods.
When we wander in the woods
we'll abandon forever all shoulds.
In the woods we'll learn how to see
as if from the top of the tallest tree.

Please say you'll come with me
to hike in the deep woods.
Your shoes might get dirty
but your spirit will fly and sing,
like an uncaged bird, a sweet melody.
You'll soar inside a pastoral symphony.

Pull yourself away and come with me,
we'll wing our way in the woods.
In the forest are no more shoulds
but only those long lost coulds.
We'll come upon hidden treasure troves
and listen to the bees buzz in the groves.

Come with me. You won't be sorry.
We'll be ourselves in the old woods,
see people from other neighborhoods
who left behind all their shoulds.
In the woods we'll go only for coulds.
Under the boughs await us rich goods.

Believe in me, come with me.
We'll go for long walks in the woods.
I swear we won't find anything bad
after leaving behind whatever is sad.
Come with me into the magical woods.
Together we'll recover forgotten goods.

Have faith in me, come with me
and I'll guide you into dark woods.
I promise to show you the old cave,

the source of the ancient stream,
and reveal what the woods gave
me when I lived there in a dream.

If you say yes and come with me,
I'll share with you my sacred woods.
When you come you'll leave behind
all the grime and the grind and find
what's beautiful but not at all tame.
Your life won't ever be the same.

Come with me, *komm' mit mir,*
we'll find our lovely lost worlds.
Under the canopy you won't fear
what kept you from coming here.
Come with me, my darling, my dear;
come away with me into the woods.

Schramm Woods

Where there was and is bog,
water squishes beneath my boots.
Mosquitoes buzz and robust
poison ivy climbs trunks
to hang out at eye level.
A white oak stretching up
beyond where I can see
is so wide it would take
many lengths of my out-
stretched arms to circle
its ancient circumference.

This rich black bog
is what saved these woods
from the axe and the plow
and the other old agricultural
machinery Jacob Schramm's
descendants left in back
corners of these woods
where two species merge
and grow together
and these man-made
machines rust back into
the black sucking earth.

One tree grows around
an axle and a pair of wheels,
lifting them up off the ground,
as if in offering to the great
gods of the primeval forest.

My wife and I stand still
under a shagbark hickory
in splotches of sunlight
and hear a splatter of rain
falling through big leaves.

She says, "I think
something is up there."
Cuttings fall on my shoulder.
I look up to trace white bits
to their source in the light
streaming through leaf clusters.

I tiptoe across dead leaves
to find an angle of vision,
as my father taught me to do
almost sixty years ago
in rolling hills to the south,
so that I can look up at
the branches and wait, wait
for the fox squirrel to climb
out to get another nut.

Finally, I see movement
and a fluffy red beneath
the fire-lit tail, cuttings fall
again, and I am there with
my father and his father
and Jacob Schramm and those
who loved this land before
he arrived, and I give thanks

for the axe that never bit
into this bark and the plow
that never cut and turned
this black boggy earth
because it was too wet
when fields were carved out,

so that I could come here,
in another time, and stand
to look up and listen and learn,
all over again, how to receive
what was given for me to praise.

Back in Indiana

1

You may find the weather extreme
and the people unseasonably mild.
Unlike the folks on the coasts,
we look you right in the eye
and speak from the interior.

Our humor can be so dry
it hits you only as you leave.
Our speech doesn't go off
like firecrackers, but our poets
sing close to the ground
and keep the fire burning.
An Indiana Isaiah must learn
to prophesy in a flat cornfield,
not from the mountaintop.

When you leave, that hum
you hear is the song
of a people in love
with where they live.

2

Back home on the ground,
we discover that the gift
the great wings gave us

is new eyes to see that
this place where we live
we love more than we knew.

back home
On the ground
We discover
that the gift
the great wings gave us
is new eyes to see that
this place where we live
we love more than we knew

Downtown Indy Freight Trains

I wake to hear them sound
their warning song, in a minor key,

in the middle of the night
as they wind their steady way

downtown through what was
once a great railway hub.

I wake to the memory of those
freight trains that wound

into my hometown, in the hills
to the south, bearing the lumber

that my father and other men
would make into chairs and desks

and cabinets. Always there were
men in those after-war years

who rode the freight trains,
wearing stubble and sadness

on their gaunt faces, and some
showed up on our porch

to ask politely for a bite to eat.
Our mother would nod and make

them a peanut butter and jelly
sandwich and hand it to them.

There was a soft light in their eyes
that stays with me, as I hear the Indy

freight train songs and also the quiet
duet the hoboes sang with my mother

as they turned to walk back toward
Buffalo Swamp to jump another freight:

"Thank you kindly, Ma'am," they said.
"Why you're welcome," she replied.

Drifting

Sometimes I awaken
in the hours before dawn,
read a few pages, reflect,

fall back asleep, drift
to a pond where I fished,
a field in which I would walk,

woods in which I could
lose myself so that I might
discover a way back out,

and I see the youthful face
of a friend I lost too soon,
hear the voices of people I loved,

and it becomes unclear
which world I live in,
which one I drift toward.

The Easter Stone Speaks

It's not that I thought I was inert
or un-alive or even dumb.
I knew I had sensation and more.

Though I did not have voice
I knew I had the power to
one day speak in my way,

even if my language had
no name. I knew there was
an energy that moved inside me,

but there never was anyone
who had the vision or intention
to make me realize my potential.

So I remained, as it was said,
dumb as a stone. To most,
if not all, I was dead to their

touch and cold as winter frost
or as hot as the summer sun.
I could absorb damp or heat

from whatever came into
contact with me. I stayed put.
But one night something

radically different touched me
from within that dark and
forbidding space where no

light had ever been seen
except from a taper. I did
my job of closing off that

space within which only
the dead dared to repose.
This touch awakened me

to the depth of my powers.
This touch spoke to the spirit
in me that until then had been

kept a secret to the world.
This time there was light
within the darkness I enclosed

that woke me to my core.
Molecules I had only sensed
were within me began to

circulate and swirl with speed.
It was as though I were pushed
from within by a source of

power and light I always
believed was in my universe
but did not have the wherewithal

to name or summon as the force
that could prove to all that I
too could be reborn into a life

that until now had never been
recognized. What I can only
call these fingertips of light

touched me in a way that
no being on any level had
ever laid such hands on me.

I moved as if of my own
volition in response to a source
of light that arose from the realm

of the dark and dreary dead. My mass
rolled away and a shape of blinding
light that was both human and not

human emerged from within
where it had been contained
and radiated outward and beyond.

The Float Forever Held

for Vince Clemente

Friend, your words
come to me again
in a distinct rhythm

I recognize at once,
as the pulse
of your spirit

stays with me
wherever you and I
go as we move on

into the next
phase of finding
where we settle

as time flows on
and we float
our words

and spirit
on the surface
of whatever waters

turn beneath
heaving us onward
toward the far shore.

End of the Path

A path led from beyond the garden
through the woods to the other side.
Beyond the woods, a patch of blackberries,
some pokeberries, and coveys of quail.

The dogs and I crossed a creek, bypassed
an old farmhouse and barn about to collapse,
came into a small woods full of squirrels,
out the other side to a persimmon tree.

My eyes absorbed how ripe the fruit was.
Not many steps more and we stood
on the banks of the Patoka, along the bottom
of which skimmed old catfish and carp.

I pulled on a long rope tied to a tree
and raised someone's trap full of flopping fish.
Mysterious light glinted off their silvery scales.
May their dark energy rise again in these lines.

Saying Patoka

Patoka, Patoka,
I say, not knowing

what the word means
but sure that it sums up

the spirits of those
who were here before

we came to their place.
Patoka, Patoka,

I say again,
wanting to conjure

water still so pure
I can step into it

and float in currents
in which spirit flows.

Moon of Falling Leaves

I am a canoe carved of tulip poplar.
It is the Moon of Falling Leaves,
and I float open on the White River
in the light of a moon that is full.

Into me fall leaves of many colors
and shapes and names that drift
together into the verses of a song
that many of this land shall sing.

These leaves of so many shapes
and hues make a rainbow of names
I ask you to sing with me as we
glide on moon-white currents

meandering toward larger waters.
Let us sing together the song
of our many different leaves
whose names make the music

of this place we love:
Miami, French, Lenape,
English, Potawatomi, Irish,
Scots, Piankashaw, German,

Hebrew, Wea, Welsh.
As I float around the bends
of this River called White,
I collect more and more falling

leaves and verse builds upon verse
in this song that shall never end:
Italian, Shawnee, African,
Latvian, Winnabago, Pole,

Slovakian, Wyandot, Chinese,
Japanese, Nanticoke, Lithuanian,
Greek, Mascouten, Asian Indian.
More leaves expand our song.

Into this poplar canoe floating
in full moonlight fall and settle
Korean, Munsee, and Belgian,
Hungarian, Kickapoo, Swiss,

more shapes and lines adding
colors, layers and texture:
Hungarian, Mexican, Vietnamese,
Colombian, Cherokee, Dutch.

Shine, Moon of Falling Leaves, shine.
Fall, multicolored leaves to come.
Flow, river, flow into deeper waters
as we sing the song we compose.

Photography Credits

All photographs are from locations in Indiana unless otherwise noted.

ii *Photo of walnut music stands that Norbert's grandfather and father made, St. Henry Church, St. Henry. March 17, 2011.*

v *Photo of Benno Krapf house, St. Henry. March 18, 2011.*

vi *Photo of Schmitt farmhouse, Ireland. March 18, 2011.*

viii *Photo of cemetery and St. Joseph Church from top of hill, Jasper. March 17, 2011.*

xii *Photo of Ohio River flood, Troy. March 18, 2011.*

xvi *Photo of daffodils by old farm machinery at Schmitt pond, Ireland. March 18, 2011.*

xviii *Photo of house on Schroeder Avenue framed by pin oak trees Norbert and his father transplanted, Jasper. March 17, 2011.*

2 *Photo of Frank Schmitt, Norbert's grandfather. Old family photo.*

5 *Photo of Dorothy Schmitt Krapf at age 25. Old family photo.*

7 *Photo of telegram to Dorothy Schmitt in Louisville during the Ohio River flood of 1937. January 29, 2011.*

11 *Photo of cedar trees where flying squirrels once flew near St. Henry Church, St. Henry. March 17, 2011.*

14 *Photo of old pamphlet featuring the two-room school that once stood at the edge of the cemetery, St. Henry. March 17, 2011.*

21 *Photo of hunter calling prey in woods, location unknown. Date unknown.*

29 *Photo of the Mayberry Café and stoplight, Danville. September 18, 2010.*

35 *Photo of steam-powered locomotive in northern Indiana. Date unknown.*

41 *Photo of barbed-wire fence, Owen County. March 12, 2011.*

43 *Photo of redbud and dogwood in bloom, Owen County. Date unknown.*

45 *Photo of Krapf family stained-glass windows in St. Henry Church, St. Henry. March 17, 2011.*

46 *Photo of pen and inkpot casting shadows on blank paper, Owen County. March 27, 2011.*

54 *Photo of draft horse in field, Monroe County. Date unknown.*

57 *Photo of corn shocks in field, Davies County. Date unknown.*

61 *Photo of hoarfrost on catalpa pods, location unknown. Date unknown.*

67 *Photo of hummingbird, Monroe County. Date unknown.*

71 *Photo of pond and old diving board pier at Schmitt family farm near Ireland. March 18, 2011.*

74 *Photo of sand and surf at Jones Beach, New York. March 22, 2011. Photo by Riley Fields.*

77 *Photo of mockingbird feather and fieldstone, Owen County. February 28, 2011.*

80 *Photo of lilac in bloom, Owen County. April 21, 2010.*

83 *Photo of Walt Whitman's birthplace, West Hills, New York. March 12, 2011. Photo by Riley Fields.*

84 *Photo of tombstone for poet Etheridge Knight at Crown Hill Cemetery, Indianapolis. March 21, 2011.*

92 *Photo of mulberry bark, Owen County. March 12, 2011.*

96 *Photo of lyre sculpted on monument at St. Joseph Church cemetery, Jasper. March 17, 2011.*

98 *Photo of Dick Adkins with hardanger fiddle, Owen County. Date unknown.*

103 *Photo of Norbert Krapf, Monika Herzig, Peter Kienle, and Carolyn Dutton at the Artsgarden, Indianapolis. March 20, 2011.*

104 *Photo of acoustic guitar with Woody Guthrie "this machine kills fascists" sticker, Owen County. March 8, 2011.*

112 *Photo of cecropia moth, Monroe County. Date unknown.*

117 *Photo of small lyre etched on monument at St. Joseph Church cemetery, Jasper. March 17, 2011.*

120 *Photo of poster for Hoosier Dylan, Indianapolis. January 29, 2011.*

130 *Photo of cap with embroidered design, Jasper. March 17, 2011.*

134 *Photo of Norbert Krapf and Gordon Bonham rehearsing, Indianapolis. September 24, 2010.*

137 *Photo of Jennie DeVoe at "Hoosier Hank and Johnny," Danville. September 18, 2010.*

139 *Photo of Greg and Kriss Ziesemer performing in Danville. September 18, 2010.*

147 *Photo of Peter Kienle playing guitar and Monika Herzig on piano at Artsgarden, Indianapolis. March 20, 2011.*

148 *Photo of leaves in creek, Putnam County. February 18, 2011.*

154 *Photo of Krapf family immigrant trunk at the Dubois County Museum, Jasper. March 19, 2011.*

159 *Photo of bubbles on Patoka River, Jasper. March 18, 2011.*

172 *Photo of organ pipes at St. Joseph Church, Jasper. March 17, 2011.*

176 *Photo of screech owls, location unknown. Date unknown.*

181 *Photo of hawk and deer carcass, Owen County. March 16, 2008.*

184 *Photo of coyote in profile, Tippecanoe County. Date unknown.*

187 *Photo of persimmons in bowl, Reelsville. Date unknown.*

189 *Photo of wild onion shoots, Jasper. March 17, 2011.*

193 *Photo of hickory shells, Owen County. March 12, 2011.*

196 *Photo of "Back Home" poem by Norbert Krapf in stained-glass window by Martin Donlin at new Indianapolis International Airport. February 27, 2011. Photo by Riley Fields.*

198 *Photo of freight train and skyline, Indianapolis. January 29, 2011.*

204 *Photo of timbers in old barn near riverwalk trail, Jasper. March 18, 2011.*

207 *Photo of White Fawn (Bessie Evans) in prayer at the Spirit of Vincennes Rendezvous, Vincennes. Date unknown.* Outdoor Indiana *magazine, photo by Richard Fields, with permission granted from Department of Natural Resources.*

208 *Photo of page from brochure showing a stained-glass window with text and fingers, St. Henry. March 17, 2011.*

212 *Photo of tops of black oak music stands made by Benno and Clarence Krapf, St. Henry Church, St. Henry. March 17, 2011.*

NORBERT KRAPF, Indiana Poet Laureate 2008–10, is English professor emeritus at Long Island University. His recent collections include *Bloodroot: Indiana Poems* (IUP, 2008) and *Invisible Presence* (IUP, 2006), *Sweet Sister Moon,* and the childhood prose memoir *The Ripest Moments.* He has released a jazz and poetry CD with Monika Herzig, *Imagine,* and as poet laureate devoted himself to reuniting poetry and music. He lives in Indianapolis.

RICHARD FIELDS is a photographer and author of *Indiana Impressions*. He is co-author of *Indiana from the Air* (IUP, 1996) and a contributor to *The Natural Heritage of Indiana* (IUP, 1998). For many years Fields was a photographer with *Outdoor Indiana* magazine. His images have also appeared in *Audubon, National Wildlife, Midwest Living, Indianapolis Monthly, Arts Indiana,* Sierra Club calendars, and National Geographic books. He resides in southern Indiana near Spencer.

This book was designed by Jamison Cockerham and set in type by Tony Brewer at Indiana University Press and printed by Integrated Book Technology, Inc.

The typeface is Warnock, designed by Robert Slimbach in 2000 and issued by Adobe Systems, Inc.